Absolute Beginner's
ORIGAMI

Absolute Beginner's
ORIGAMI

The Simple Three-Stage Guide
to Creating Expert Origami

Nick Robinson

APPLE

A QUARTO BOOK

Copyright © 1999, 2002 by
Quarto Publishing plc

Published by Apple Press
Sheridan House
112-116A Western Road
Hove
East Sussex BN3 1DD

Reprinted 2002

ISBN 1-84092-165-X

This book was designed and produced by
Quarto Publishing plc
The Old Brewery
6 Blundell Street
London N7 9BH

Project editor Marnie Haslam
Editor Mike Stocks
Art editor Suzanne Metcalfe-Megginson
Designer Kevin Williams
Photography Martin Norris, Andrew Sydenham
Illustrator Terry Evans
Art director Moira Clinch
Assistant art director Penny Cobb
QUAR.AGO

Manufactured in Hong Kong by Regent Publishing
Services Ltd.
Printed in China by Leefung-Asco Printers Ltd.

CONTENTS

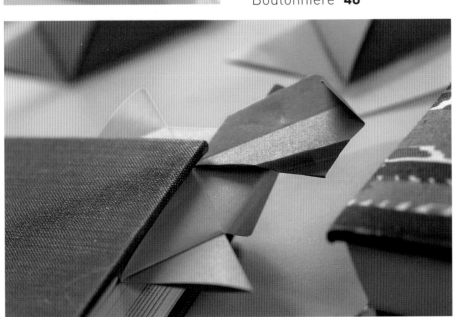

HOW TO USE THIS BOOK

ORIGAMI is the art of folding paper to produce lifelike, decorative, or even abstract designs. Most origami models start with a very simple folding sequence known as a base. The key to successful paperfolding is to understand the basic folding techniques, then to expand on your knowledge and expertise from there!

STAGE 1—BASIC TECHNIQUES

- Learn the basic folding techniques listed as "folds" and "bases."
- Follow the step-by-step instructions accompanied by color photographs.
- Practice each technique many times until you are confident.

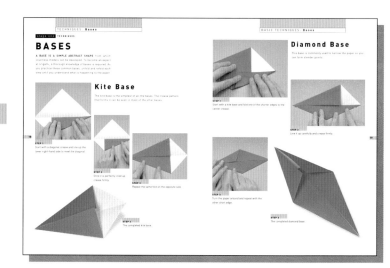

STAGE 2—PRACTICE PIECES

- Make simple origami models using the basic techniques learned in Stage 1.
- Follow the step-by-step instructions using a practice sheet of paper.
- The panel of illustrations at the bottom of the page will remind you how to make the base.
- See the Help! box for additional advice.
- Practice each design until you are confident.
- Ten sheets of practice paper with printed fold lines are provided for this stage.

STAGE 3—PROJECT

- Tackle the projects with confidence as you follow the step-by-step instructions.
- Don't forget to refer to the "reminder" panel at the bottom of the page and the Help! box, if you need assistance.
- A special sheet of colored origami paper is provided for each project.

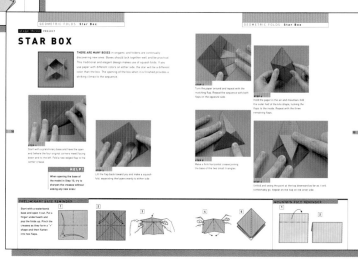

MATERIALS & EQUIPMENT

Of all the crafts or arts you might try, origami is, without doubt, the most economical—all you need is a piece of paper and your hands! In addition to a supply of paper, a well-lit desktop or table makes folding easier. As you build up a small collection of origami books, a bookshelf will become necessary. You can then display your best work on top of it.

Commercially available paper should be perfectly square, but if you buy larger sheets of paper, you will need to cut them down to size. There are two basic methods of doing this:

- Use a papercutter. This should be as big as possible for producing larger squares. Papercutters make life very easy, but they can be expensive.

- Use a craft knife on a cutting mat. The knife should have a retractable blade for safety reasons—some have "snap-off" blades, which are ideal. Cutting mats are inexpensive, and readily available at most craft shops.

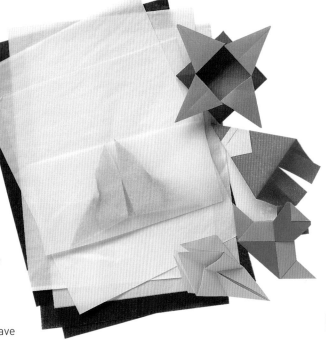

7

STORING YOUR ORIGAMI
Storing origami is a problem for experts and beginners alike. The most common solution is to wrap pieces carefully in tissue paper and keep them in a cardboard box.

CUTTING PAPER
Always be very careful when cutting paper, and if using a knife, safely store it away after use. To produce a square from a rectangle is not difficult—simply follow these three steps:

STEP 1
Start with a corner of the rectangle.

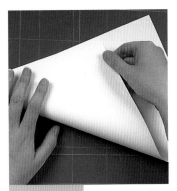

STEP 2
Fold the corner over to create a triangle. Line up the top edges evenly.

STEP 3
Trim off the remainder.

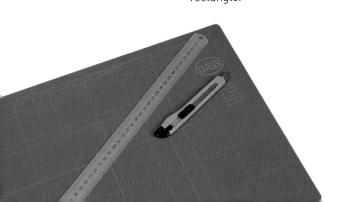

Selecting Paper

The type of paper you use to fold with will depend on what you want to do with the finished piece. If you are folding a model for the first time, plain paper will be fine. If you are going to exhibit your work in an art gallery or library, you will need to carefully consider the size, color, weight, and texture of the paper.

SIZE

The nature of paperfolding means that your end result will be many times smaller than the sheet of paper. If you want a finished model of a specific size, you will have to fold it first from a sample size of paper to see by how much it reduces. You can then work out how big your sheet of paper will need to be to produce the size of model you desire. Folding very large or very small models is very challenging, and an art in itself. However, with a little patience and practice, you will soon achieve the desired result.

COLOR AND PATTERN

Beginners will often fold from brightly colored paper regardless of the subject. Once you have mastered a particular design (which may mean folding it many, many times), you can then decide which color or pattern will suit it best. Remember, the choice is yours! Try not to use extremely bright colors that may distract from the model itself. A beautifully folded origami model should be impressive even when made from plain brown wrapping paper.

WEIGHT

The weight or thickness of the paper will determine which models you can fold from it. Complex folds are not suited to thick paper, since you won't be able to produce thin points or sometimes even fold the paper in half without tearing it! Thin paper may not be sturdy enough for models that rely on the strength of the paper to keep their shape. Standard photocopy paper is an ideal weight for folding, and you can buy it very cheaply.

TEXTURE

Thicker paper often has a distinct texture or feel to it. This can enhance the look of certain models and can add a pleasing tactile appeal to your finished design.

STANDARD ORIGAMI PAPER

On this page is a selection of sheets from a typical pack of origami paper. The sheets usually come in a wide assortment of colors, and measure 6 inches (15 cm) square, an ideal size for folding most designs.

Paper Types

FOIL PAPER (below)
Gold and silver are popular
colors, but experience is
required for the best results.

ORIGAMI PAPER

Most origami paper has a colored side and a plain white side, although you can find paper colored on both sides. A typical pack of paper contains sheets in several colors measuring 6 inches (15 cm) square, but other sizes are also sold. Over the past few years, an exciting range of patterns and finishes have been made available. Washi paper is handmade in Japan and uses a variety of traditional patterns and designs. The paper itself is quite soft in texture and is not suited to complex designs, but Washi paper will lend your work an authentic Oriental charm.

FOIL PAPER

You may have used this paper during arts and crafts at school—a sheet of white paper backed with a layer of shiny foil. You can find it in a variety of colors, although gold and silver are the most common. The larger rolls of foil paper are smooth, but you can buy many different embossed textures designed especially for origami. Kitchen foil is not suitable on its own, although some folders use spray-mount adhesive to glue a layer of tissue to either side of the aluminum foil. This laminate is known as "tissue-foil-tissue" and allows for very small, complex designs to be folded. All types of foil suffer from a serious drawback: It is almost impossible to change the direction of a crease once it is made.

WRAPPING PAPER

Most wrapping papers are excellent for folding, although you will usually need to cut them into smaller squares.

RECYCLED PAPER

The cheaper type of recycled paper is not suitable for folding, since it doesn't retain a sharp crease very well. In the best traditions of recycling, however, you will be able to find and reuse a huge range of papers such as handouts, computer paper, leaflets, posters, tickets, and many others. These are usually free and are ideal materials for practicing your designs.

PATTERNED AND WRAPPING PAPER (below and right)
Achieve a unique or attractive look with patterned or wrapping paper. If it is only available in large sheets, simply cut it down to size.

START FOLDING

WHEN TO FOLD

The key to successful folding is taking your time. As with many activities, work that is done in a hurry is not usually very satisfying. Set aside sufficient time so that you don't feel rushed. Also, try to choose a time when you will have some peace and quiet; it's hard to work out difficult moves with lots of background noise. Some folders find that relaxing music helps them concentrate.

WHERE TO FOLD

Use a table with enough space for you to open the book and still have plenty of room for the paper and your elbows. Natural light is perhaps the best, but whatever lighting you use, make sure there is plenty of it. If you can arrange it so that the light is slightly to one side, the creases on the paper will show up more clearly.

HOW TO FOLD

Origami creases need to be made neatly and accurately; this is achieved by lining the paper up carefully and slowly before creasing. A few more seconds spent adjusting the paper will lead to a much more impressive result. When you progress to making complex designs, a small mistake on the first crease may mean that you can't finish the model!

Try to be aware of how the paper wants to behave; if you have to force it, you may be doing something wrong. If a crease begins to crumple, unfold that step immediately, flatten the paper, and try again, more gently.

USING THE SYMBOLS

One reason why origami has such an international appeal is because its folding instructions use a standard set of symbols. These symbols were created by the origami master Akira Yoshizawa and refined by an American, Samuel Randlett. The use of these symbols means that people all over the world can follow the instructions, regardless of the language they speak. The basic set of symbols is small, although many new symbols have been introduced over the years.

10

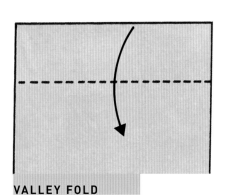

VALLEY FOLD
Shown above by a series of dashes—
one side of the paper folds up and over.

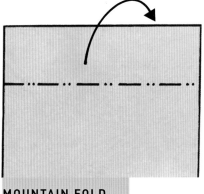

MOUNTAIN FOLD
Shown above by a dash and two dots—
one side of the paper folds underneath
the other.

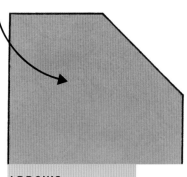

ARROWS
Shown above indicating the
direction of the folding action.

BASIC FOLDS

FOLDING TECHNIQUES are the heart of origami. There is a logical progression to following the basic folds, and it is essential that you spend enough time practicing them until they come naturally to you. Once you have mastered these folds, you can begin to combine them into your own original creations!

Below and on pages 12-17 are the basic folding techniques you will need to complete the projects in this book. You should practice each fold using scrap paper until you thoroughly understand how it works. As you practice, alter distances and angles to see how they affect the end result.

Valley Fold

The valley fold is the fundamental starting point for all origami. Since it is a simple fold, try to make it perfect every time.

STEP 1

Lift one edge of the paper and fold it over to the opposite edge.

11

STEP 2

Line up the edges slowly and carefully—try to keep the lower half still and only move the top half.

STEP 3

Hold the layers in place with one hand and flatten the crease with the other, starting from the center and creasing outward (not shown). When you open up this fold, the raised sides of the paper will form a valley.

Mountain Fold

A mountain fold is the opposite of a valley fold. Since it is difficult to fold paper away from you and line it up neatly, you can turn the paper over and make a valley fold, then turn it over again to reverse the fold to make a mountain fold.

STEP 1

After making a valley fold, turn the paper over. Lift the bottom edge of the paper and fold it to meet the opposite edge using the same fold line, but changing the direction of the crease.

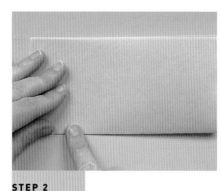

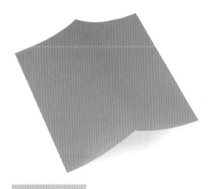

STEP 2

Make a firm crease along the fold line.

STEP 3

If you unfold the paper and set it on the table, the crease should form a distinct ridge that gives the fold a "mountain" appearance.

12

Location Crease

Sometimes you will need to make a fold that does not line up with an edge or corner. To do this we create a small crease known as a location crease. For example, you may need to fold to the center of a square but without making too many unnecessary creases.

STEP 1

Start with a sheet that has been vertically folded in half and unfolded again. Then fold the bottom of the sheet toward the top, but do not flatten the paper!

STEP 2

Line up the paper carefully, as if you were making a full crease, but instead, make a very small, gentle crease at the center.

STEP 3

Open out to reveal the location crease. The point where it meets the original crease is the center of the paper.

Squash Fold

This technique is very common in origami and its name is highly appropriate! If a squash fold starts to crumple, unfold it immediately, flatten the paper, and try again.

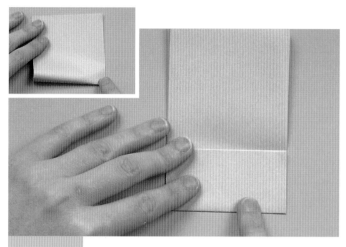

STEP 1

Start with a square that has been folded in half from left to right. Fold the bottom short edge to the opposite edge, but don't flatten the crease.

STEP 2

Make a small location crease at the halfway point (see inset), then unfold. Fold the same short edge to meet the location point and crease firmly.

STEP 3

Now lift the flap you have just made and start to open the two layers.

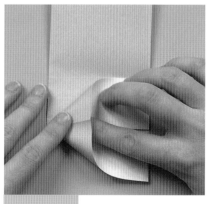

STEP 4

Slide your finger up between the layers until it meets the end. As your finger moves up, the top point of the flap will start to flatten outward. Put a finger on top of it and encourage it to flatten evenly. Use the center crease to make sure that it is lined up.

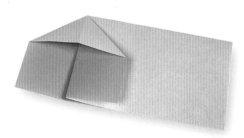

STEP 5

The completed squash fold.

Rabbit's Ear

This technique uses three separate creases to form a small triangular flap that can swing to both sides. It is often used to create ears, hence the name.

STEP 1
Fold one corner to the opposite corner, forming a triangle. Place a finger in the center of the folded edge and start to crease outward.

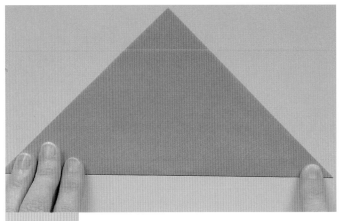

STEP 2
The completed diagonal crease.

14

STEP 3
Unfold the paper, then fold the lower left-hand edge to meet the diagonal crease along the center of the paper.

STEP 4
Crease it firmly and unfold.

STEP 5
Now repeat Steps 3 and 4 on the lower right-hand side and unfold.

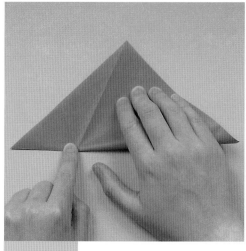

STEP 6

Rotate your paper 90-degrees clockwise and fold in half, but only crease outward from the left diagonal fold (as shown above).

STEP 7

Unfold and rotate your paper counter-clockwise back to the same position of Step 5. Lift the bottom left- and right-hand sides upward and fold inward.

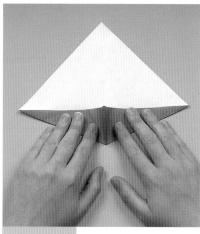

STEP 8

This will cause the central flap to point upward.

15

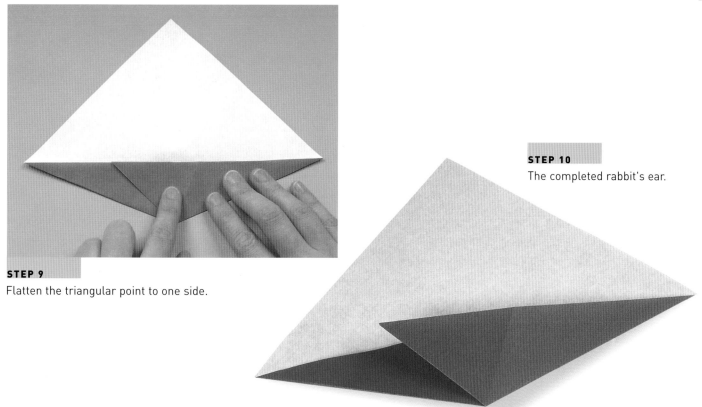

STEP 9

Flatten the triangular point to one side.

STEP 10

The completed rabbit's ear.

Inside Reverse

This fold is called the inside reverse fold because you have to "reverse" two of its three creases. Since the paper moves inside, it becomes an inside reverse fold. The secret to a successful fold is to make the pre-crease in Step 3 firmly and neatly.

STEP 1

Start with a kite base (see page 18). Fold in half along the center crease...

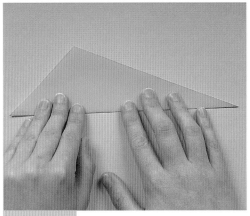

STEP 2

...like this.

STEP 3

Fold part of the sharp end at an angle, away from the long folded edge. The exact angle isn't important. Crease firmly.

STEP 4

Unfold back to Step 1 and turn the paper around. All the creases for the reverse fold are present but some need to change direction. Fold the paper down using the lower of the two short creases. The paper won't lie flat at this stage.

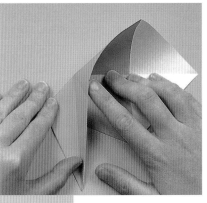

STEP 5

The original diagonal crease becomes a valley crease. The other short crease also has to change direction as the paper flattens down.

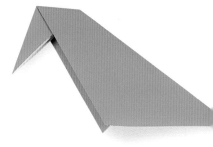

STEP 6

Reinforce the creases to complete the inside reverse fold.

Outside Reverse

This technique is similar to the inside reverse fold, but as you will see, once the fold is completed the "reversed" paper will lie on the outside.

STEP 1

Start with a kite base (see page 18), folded in half as you did for the inside reverse fold. This time, swing the point at an angle away from the double-folded edge and flatten firmly. Note that this is the opposite direction to Step 3 of the inside reverse fold.

STEP 2

Open out to the underside of the kite base. One of the short creases is a valley (which we need); the other, a mountain crease, must be changed into a valley.

STEP 3

Start to fold the paper in half along the original diagonal, putting the short valley crease into place. The center crease of the reversed point also has to change direction.

17

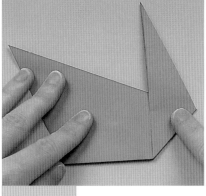

STEP 4

Here is the same fold shown from another angle. You can see how all three of the creases that make the reversed point become valley creases.

STEP 5

Flatten all the creases.

STEP 6

The completed outside reverse fold.

stage one **TECHNIQUES**

BASES

A BASE IS A SIMPLE ABSTRACT SHAPE from which countless models can be developed. To become an expert at origami, a thorough knowledge of bases is required. As you practice these common bases, unfold and refold each step until you understand what is happening to the paper.

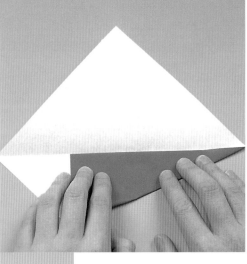

Kite Base

The kite base is the simplest of all the bases. The crease pattern that forms it can be seen in most of the other bases.

STEP 1
Start with a diagonal crease and line up the lower right-hand side to meet the diagonal.

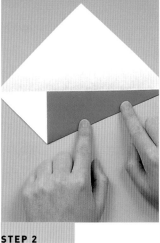

STEP 2
Once it is perfectly lined up, crease firmly.

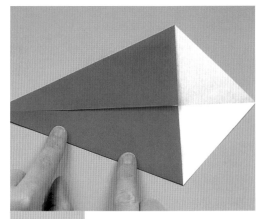

STEP 3
Repeat the same fold on the opposite side.

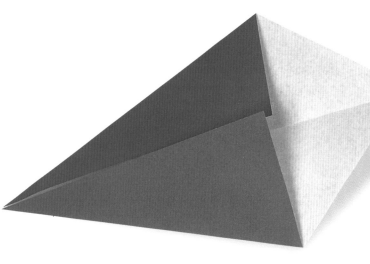

STEP 4
The completed kite base.

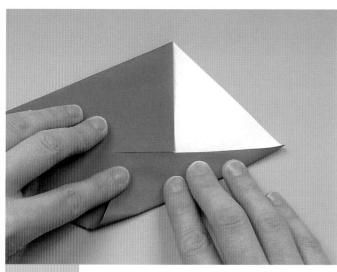

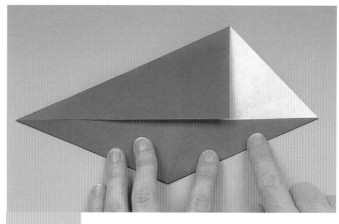

Diamond Base

This base is commonly used to narrow the paper so you can form slender points.

STEP 1

Start with a kite base and fold one of the shorter edges to the center crease.

STEP 2

Line it up carefully and crease firmly.

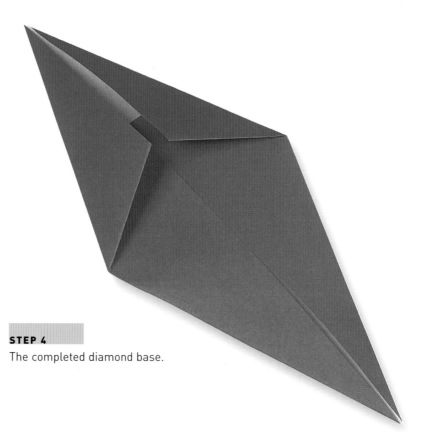

STEP 3

Turn the paper around and repeat with the other short edge.

STEP 4

The completed diamond base.

Fish Base

The fish base is formed by creating two rabbit's ears on either side of a square. These flaps can then be squash- and petal-folded to form, for instance, legs.

STEP 1

Start with an upside-down kite base, sharp point toward you. Fold the sharp point to the opposite end...

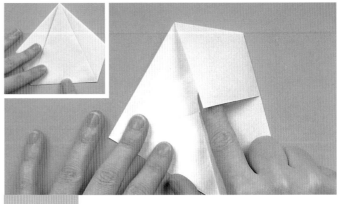

STEP 2

...and crease firmly (see inset). Turn the paper over and rotate it slightly. Put a finger inside one of the pockets and begin to open it up...

 20

STEP 3

...so that the two raw edges line up along the center crease...

STEP 4

...like this. Flatten the paper neatly.

STEP 5

Repeat Steps 2-4 on the other side, making sure the raw edges line up neatly.

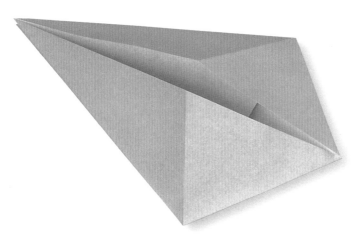

STEP 6

The completed fish base.

Waterbomb Base

This is the classic base for making the waterbomb that is familiar to many schoolchildren. If you turn it inside out, the same creases form a preliminary base.

STEP 1

Start with the intended base color facing upward. Fold the square in half and unfold.

STEP 2

Then fold the square in half from left to right and unfold.

STEP 3

Turn the paper over to the other side and fold it from corner to corner to create a diagonal crease. Open and fold the opposite diagonal.

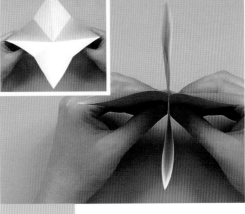

STEP 4

These are all the creases you need (see inset). Hold the paper underneath and gently press toward the center. The paper should easily fold into a star shape.

STEP 5

Flatten the paper so that there are two flaps on either side of the center fold. Reinforce the creases.

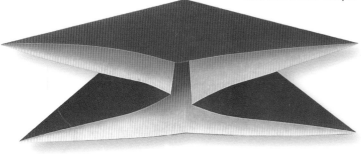

STEP 6

The completed waterbomb base.

Preliminary Base

The four corners of the square meet together in this base. It has proven to be an inspiring starting point for folders.

STEP 1

Start with a waterbomb base and begin to open it out.

STEP 2

When nearly open, put a finger underneath the center of the paper...

STEP 3

...and "pop" the creases inside out.

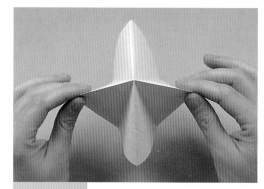

STEP 4

Finally, pinch the mountain creases on either side and begin to press these downward and together.

STEP 5

The paper will form into a shape like the flight of a dart. Flatten the paper so that there are two flaps on either side of the center fold.

STEP 6

The completed preliminary base.

22

Frog Base

This classic base provides an excellent opportunity to practice a number of folds.

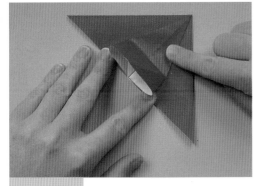

STEP 1
Start with a waterbomb base (see page 21), with the open pocket toward you. Fold the bottom left-hand corner upward to meet the top corner.

STEP 2
Fold the top left edge in again to meet the center. Crease firmly and neatly!

STEP 3
Return the paper to its original position in Step 1. Slide your finger under the first layer and begin to lift and squash fold it evenly toward the center using the creases that are already present.

23

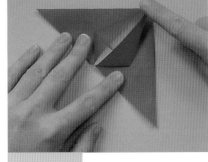

STEP 4
When the flap is squashed halfway, lift the tip of the bottom flap toward the top point, folding it at the horizontal crease. Allow the sides to fold inward...

STEP 5
...making a petal fold (similar to that used in the bird base, see page 24).

STEP 6
Flatten all the creases neatly. Repeat all steps on the other three corners.

STEP 7
The completed frog base.

`stage one` **TECHNIQUES**

Bird Base

This base has a delightful sequence of folds, creating four independent points that can be used to create a huge variety of subjects.

STEP 1

Start with a preliminary base, rotated so that the folded corner point is at the top. Fold the lower left-hand layer so that it lines up with the center crease.

STEP 2

Repeat on the right-hand side. Turn the paper over and repeat the same two folds.

STEP 3

Turn the paper around and fold the triangular flap upward...

STEP 4

...and crease firmly.

STEP 5

Turn the paper over from top to bottom and open the two top flaps (Steps 1 and 2) out again.

STEP 6

Then, lift the top layer up by the loose corner, holding the other flaps flat to the table...

STEP 7

...and swing it upward so that it starts to flatten on either side.

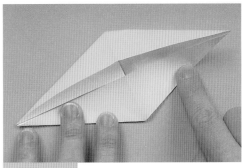

STEP 8

You will need to carefully change the direction of two creases as you flatten the sides.

STEP 9

Reinforce all the creases. You have just completed a "petal fold."

STEP 10

Turn the paper over and release the left and right flaps from underneath the triangular flap.

STEP 11

Lift the top flap upward and flatten as you did in Steps 6 to 9.

25

STEP 12

Both sides are now petal-folded. Then, fold both upper flaps down again.

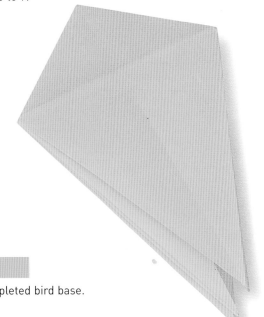

STEP 13

The completed bird base.

STEP 1

Start with a square which has been folded in half both ways and unfolded. Fold the one edge to the center crease. Repeat this fold on the opposite edge so that both opposite edges now meet in the center of the paper.

Windmill Base

This base differs from the others in that the corners form triangular flaps that can be swung to either side. This allows for a variety of shapes to be created with minimal effort.

STEP 2

Turn the paper sideways and fold the shorter edge to the center crease.

26

STEP 3

Turn the paper around and repeat with the opposite short edge, flattening carefully.

STEP 4

Rotate the paper 90-degrees and fold the bottom right-hand edge over to meet the vertical folded edge. Repeat on the three other edges.

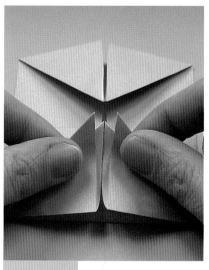

STEP 5

Hold the folded paper so that one set of triangles is facing you (as shown above), then lift a triangular flap upward, holding each side loosely between your finger and thumb.

STEP 6

Ease the outer layers away from each other, so that the inner triangle moves toward the center of the square.

STEP 7

Continue pulling the two triangular flaps to the side until they come free.

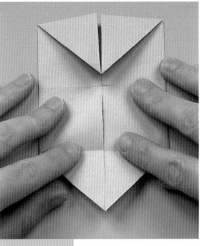

STEP 8

The paper flattens neatly and the two flaps fold downward to form a point. Repeat Steps 5 to 8 on the other end.

27

STEP 9

Crease firmly to reinforce the new folds.

STEP 10

The completed windmill base.

STAR

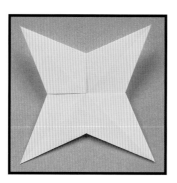

THE BIRD BASE is over one hundred years old and has proved to be very versatile, as it can be used to create a wide variety of subjects, including birds, snails, and people. This base is also suitable for creating several types of stars. The more advanced of these are three dimensional, but many, including the example here, are flat. This traditional design is ideal for practicing neat creasing and folding.

When making the squash fold, try to work with the paper rather than force it. If it starts to crumple, open the paper, flatten it, and try again. The fold lines for this design have been provided on one of the practice sheets.

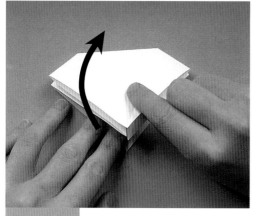

STEP 1

Make a bird base with the color inside as far as Step 5. Hold the lower layer flat to the table and lift the upper layer of paper, swinging it all the way over so it lies flat. This will cause the two inner flaps of the middle layer to point upward.

STEP 2

Put a finger inside one of the inner flaps and squash-fold it...

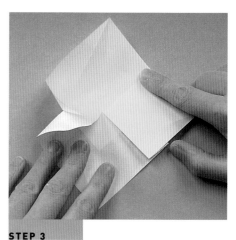

STEP 3

...flattening carefully and evenly to either side. Repeat on the opposite side.

BIRD BASE REMINDER

Start with a preliminary base. After Step 2, turn over and repeat. Unfold the two flaps to complete Step 5.

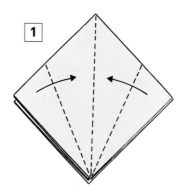

1

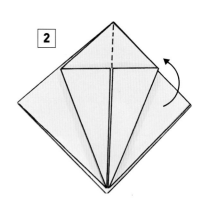

2

28

STEP 4

Turn the paper over and rotate it to the position shown. Fold one of the raw edges to the diagonal crease using an existing crease.

STEP 5

As it folds in, it will start to bring an adjoining edge with it. A new crease is formed pointing to the center as you carefully flatten the paper.

STEP 6

Make the same fold on the side to the right...

STEP 7

...and repeat on the remaining two raw edges. Flatten all the creases. Turn the paper over.

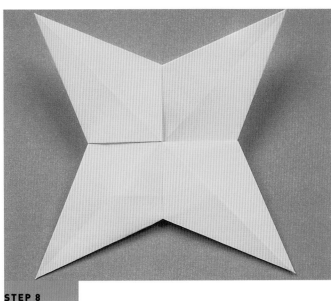

STEP 8

The completed star.

29

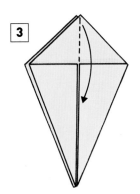

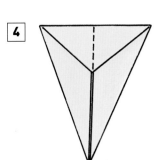

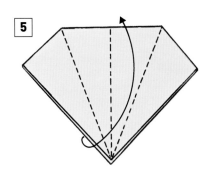

STAR RING

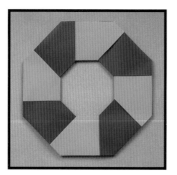

DUE TO THE SUPERB WORK of origami artist Tomoko Fuse, the last few years have seen a huge interest in modular origami. This type of folding uses identical units or modules, each folded from a single sheet of paper, which are then combined to form eye-catching two-, or three-dimensional designs. The fold lines for this design have been provided on one of the practice sheets.

Modular folding needs to be accurate or the final result may not hold together properly. Once you have mastered the technique of assembly, try using different-colored squares to vary the pattern.

30

STEP 1

Start with a square of paper that has been vertically folded in half. Fold a corner in to meet the crease (see inset). Repeat with the matching corner on the other side of the crease. Fold the square in half using the existing crease.

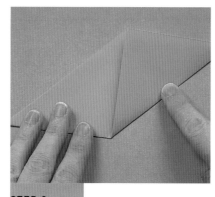

STEP 2

Fold a short edge to lie along the other short edge. Crease firmly and unfold back to the beginning of Step 2.

STEP 3

Inside reverse-fold the corner using the creases made in the last step.

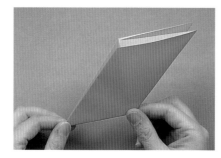

STEP 4

The module is complete. Make seven more units.

INSIDE REVERSE FOLD REMINDER

Start with a kite base. All necessary folds are present by Step 5, but they must change direction. Ease the paper gently back along the fold lines to "reverse" the fold.

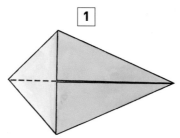

1

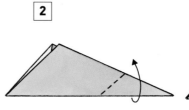

2

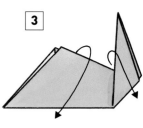

3

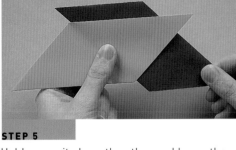

STEP 5

Hold one unit above the other and lower the higher unit between the two open edges of the lower unit as shown.

STEP 6

Make sure it is tightly inserted, then tuck a small overlapping flap behind into the "pocket" of the second unit.

STEP 7

Repeat with the overlapping flap from behind, keeping both units tightly interlocked.

STEP 8

Continue adding units, making sure they are all tightly inserted. The final unit is a little difficult, but perfectly possible if you are careful.

HELP!

If the final model is flimsy, you need to make sure the assembly is as tight as possible when adding each unit.

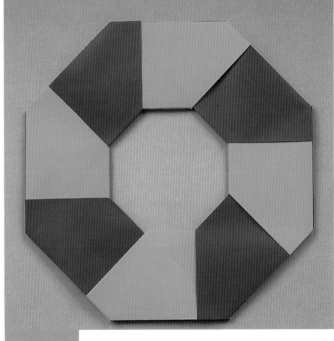

STEP 9

The model is finished. You have two choices: either slide all the units away from each other to form an octagonal ring, or slide them into each other to form an attractive star.

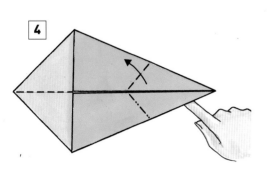

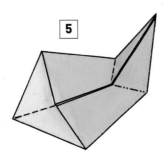

STAR BOX

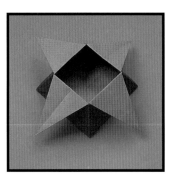

THERE ARE MANY BOXES in origami, and folders are continually discovering new ones. Boxes should lock together well and be practical. This traditional and elegant design makes use of squash folds. If you use paper with different colors on either side, the star will be a different color than the box. The opening of the box when it is finished provides a striking climax to the sequence.

STEP 1

Start with a preliminary base and have the open end (where the four original corners meet) facing down and to the left. Fold a raw-edged flap to the center crease.

HELP!

When opening the base of the model in Step 10, try to sharpen the creases without adding any new ones!

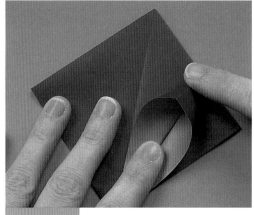

STEP 2

Lift the flap back toward you and make a squash-fold, separating the layers evenly to either side.

PRELIMINARY BASE REMINDER

Start with a waterbomb base and open it out. Put a finger underneath and pop the folds up. Pinch the creases as they form a "+" shape and then flatten into two flaps.

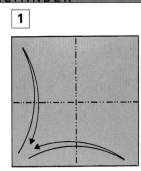

1

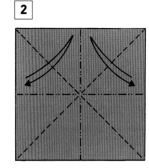

2

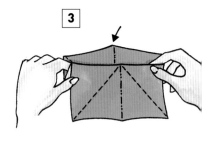

3

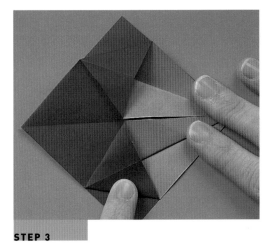

STEP 3

Turn the paper around and repeat with the matching flap. Repeat the sequence with both flaps on the opposite side.

STEP 4

Hold the paper in the air and mountain-fold the outer half of the kite shape, tucking the flaps to the inside. Repeat with the three remaining flaps.

STEP 5

Make a firm horizontal crease joining the base of the two small triangles.

STEP 6

Unfold and swing the point at the top downward as far as it will comfortably go. Repeat on the flap on the other side.

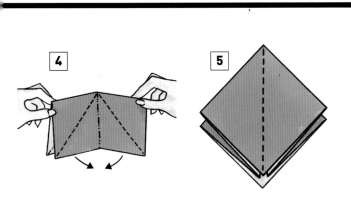

4

5

MOUNTAIN FOLD REMINDER

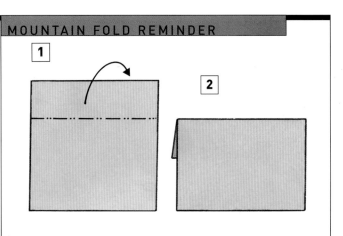

1

2

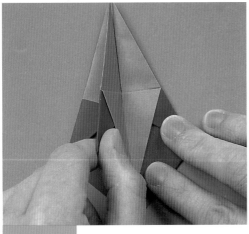

STEP 7

Fold the left-hand flap to the right...

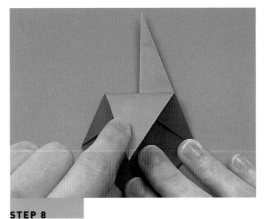

STEP 8

...and swing the upper point downward as far as it will go.

STEP 9

Fold the right flap to the left and repeat on the remaining point.

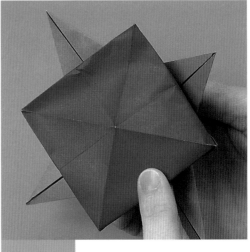

STEP 10

Nearly there now! Turn the paper upside down, place a finger inside the opening, then start to flatten the base into a neat square. Pinch the edges to help flatten the paper. Sharpen the creases around the base, turn the paper over, and you have a star box!

34

SQUASH FOLD REMINDER

Start with a square that has been folded in half. After folding to center, separate the two layers and "squash" the fold. Be sure to line up the squashed fold with the center crease.

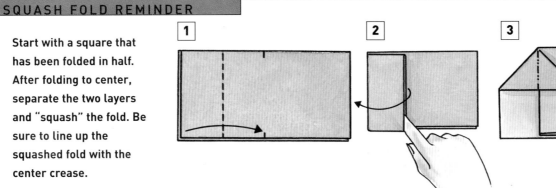

stage two **PRACTICE PIECE**

SWAN

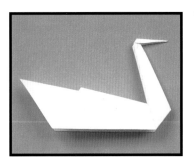

THE FLOWING LINES and pure white color of the swan has inspired folders for many years. This design is a simple, traditional model that uses two reverse folds to create the neck and head. The fold lines for this design have been provided on one of the practice sheets, but feel free to experiment with different proportions to create your own design.

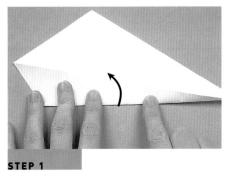

STEP 1
Start with an upside-down kite base. Fold a long edge to the center crease.

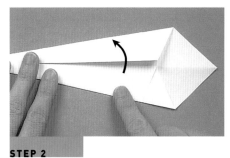

STEP 2
Turn the paper around and repeat with the other long edge.

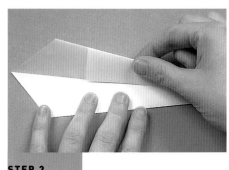

STEP 3
Mountain-fold the model in half along the center crease.

36

STEP 4
Starting at a point about halfway along the lower edge, swing the sharp point upward so that it angles back slightly.

HELP!

When narrowing paper to a sharp point, you should take extra time to line the paper up carefully, or you may end up with a blunt beak.

KITE BASE REMINDER

Start with a diagonal crease and fold one side in to line up with the center crease. Repeat on the other side.

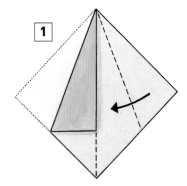

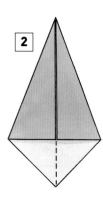

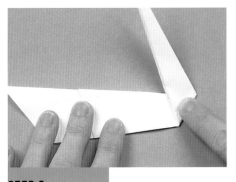

STEP 5

This will be the neck. Press the crease firmly and unfold.

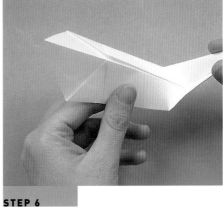

STEP 6

Open the two layers underneath the model and use the creases made in the last step to make an outside reverse fold.

STEP 7

Reinforce the reverse fold.

STEP 8

Fold the tip of the point forward to form a beak, crease firmly, and unfold.

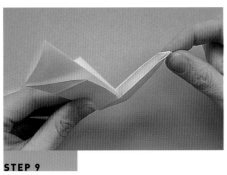

STEP 9

Using the last crease, make another outside reverse-fold.

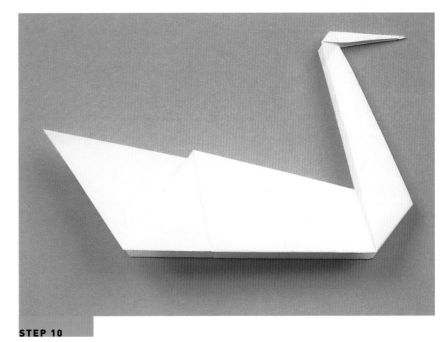

STEP 10

The completed swan.

37

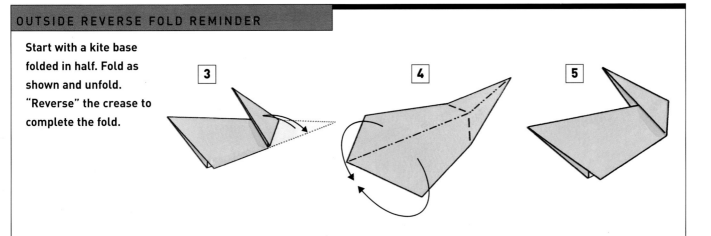

OUTSIDE REVERSE FOLD REMINDER

Start with a kite base folded in half. Fold as shown and unfold. "Reverse" the crease to complete the fold.

3

4

5

IRIS

THE FROG BASE can be used to make one or two classic designs—including the frog itself—but this iris is the most elegant and beautiful. The base is relatively complex because it is smaller than most other bases, so fold carefully! You can make use of a well-known paper-curling technique to encourage the petals to curve outward and downward.

Flower folds are an ideal opportunity to experiment with more exotic types of patterned paper.

HELP!

A neat result depends largely on accurate creasing, so take your time. Start with a larger square, then gradually reduce the size.

38

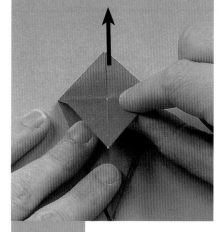

STEP 1
Start with a frog base, colored side outward. Lift all four loose flaps to point upward.

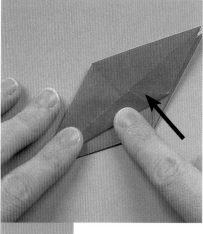

STEP 2
Narrow the lower side by folding the edge to the center.

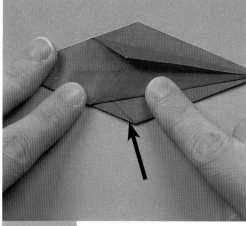

STEP 3
Turn the paper around and fold the matching edge in as well.

FROG BASE REMINDER

Start with a waterbomb base. Fold a bottom corner up, fold it in to the center again and unfold. Lift the flap, squash fold it halfway and make a petal fold. Repeat on all three corners.

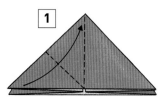

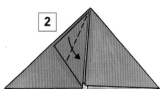

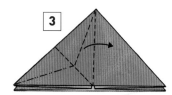

STEP 4

Repeat the last two steps on the three other flaps around the model.

STEP 5

Fold the top flap down as far as it will comfortably go. Repeat with the other three flaps.

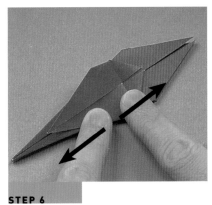

STEP 6

Gently pull these two flaps apart.

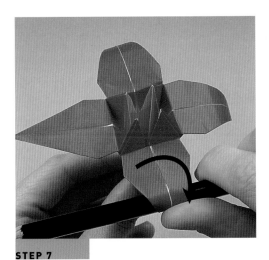

STEP 7

Wind each petal around a pencil so that they curl downward.

STEP 8

The completed iris.

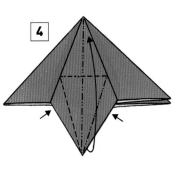

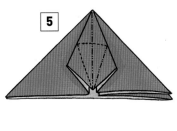

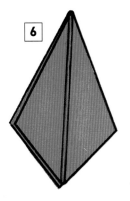

BUTTERFLY

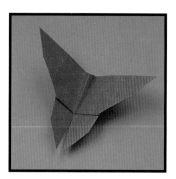

BUTTERFLIES are another popular subject for folders. Made from small squares of brightly colored paper, they can sometimes seem almost real. Try to fold with a light touch, or the model will look clumsy and heavy. The idea is to aim for a light, delicate appearance. The windmill base from which the butterfly is formed can be used for a large number of subjects.

Try swinging the windmill flaps in different directions to see if you can discover a new design "hidden" in the paper!

STEP 1

Start with a windmill base. Mountain-fold the top half of the paper behind.

HELP!

Keep the body of the butterfly firmly on the table when adding the body crease (Step 9).

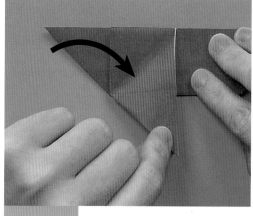

STEP 2

Swing a flap downward.

WINDMILL BASE REMINDER

Start with a preliminary base opened out. Follow the simple folding steps until Step 5. Pull the triangular flaps until the paper flattens and forms a point on each side.

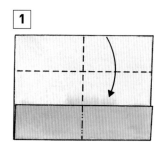

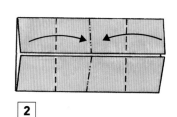

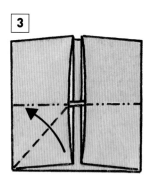

40

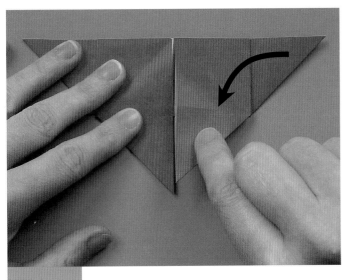

STEP 3

Repeat with the other flap.

STEP 4

To narrow the lower wing, fold in a corner.

STEP 5

Repeat on the other side.

STEP 6

Shape the upper wings in a similar fashion.

41

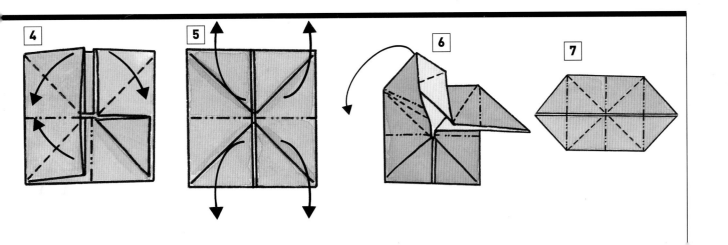

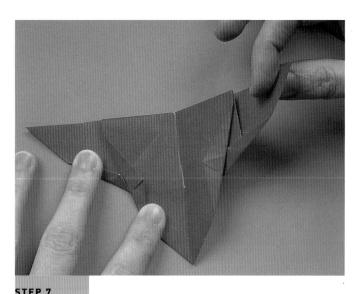

STEP 7

Valley-fold the model in half from right to left.

STEP 8

Then, valley-fold the top wing back at a slight angle.

STEP 9

Crease firmly and turn the paper over.

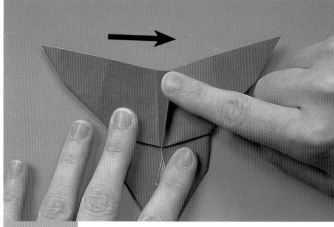

STEP 10

Swing the central flap to the right to reinforce it, then leave it pointing upward.

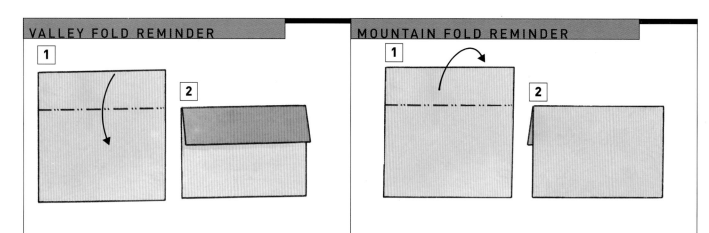

VALLEY FOLD REMINDER

1

2

MOUNTAIN FOLD REMINDER

1

2

WALLET

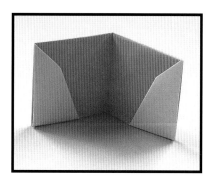

ORIGAMI is wonderful for making small, practical objects. Here is a small wallet in which you can keep money, photos, or even postage stamps, if you make it small enough! Try to choose a paper that is durable, so you can use it for many months. This design could make an ideal present for a friend. The fold lines for this design have been provided on one of the practice sheets.

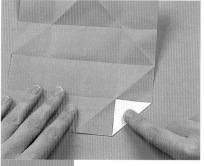

STEP 1
Start with a windmill base, opened back out to the square. Valley-fold a corner to meet the intersection of three creases.

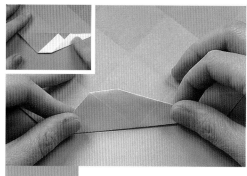

STEP 2
Fold half of the lower raw edge to meet the 45-degree crease (see inset)...then swing the whole corner in on that crease (main picture).

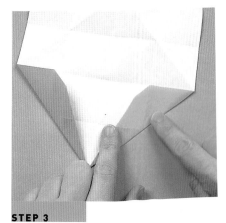

STEP 3
Rotate your paper to the left and repeat all the steps on the adjacent corner.

44

HELP!

When tucking the final flap inside, let the paper "curl" into the pocket rather than forcing it in (Step 8).

WINDMILL BASE REMINDER

Start with a preliminary base opened back to the square. Follow the simple folding steps until Step 5. Then pull the triangular flaps at one end until the paper flattens and forms a point. Repeat on other end.

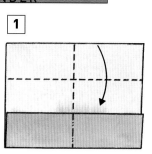

1

2

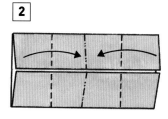

3

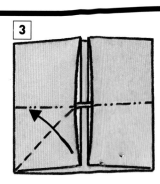

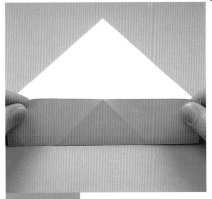

STEP 4

Turn the paper over. Fold the long raw edge down to the center crease.

STEP 5

Fold both of the short sides in to the center crease.

STEP 6

Turn the paper over, keeping the point at the top. Using an existing crease, valley-fold the bottom section away from you.

STEP 7

Turn the paper around again, then tuck the corner inside the pocket formed in Step 6. Make sure it folds in completely.

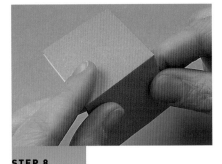

STEP 8

Mountain-fold the model in half down the center.

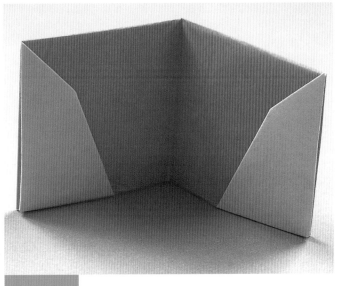

STEP 9

The completed wallet.

45

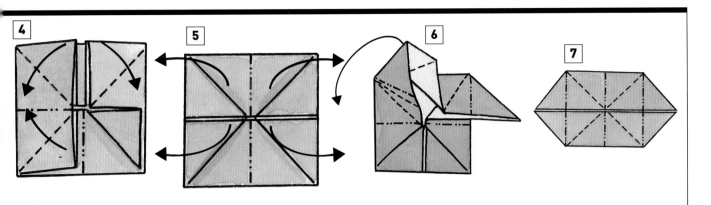

HEART

THE SINGAPORE FOLDER Francis Ow has written several books that deal solely with origami hearts. This design has a pleasing three-dimensional aspect and is also practical, since you can wear it by tucking it into a breast pocket.

The technique that allows us to create the shape of the heart is known as a "butterfly" lock, and it is an elegant method often used to make three-dimensional designs.

46

STEP 1

Start with a kite base folded with the colored side out. Fold the sharp corner to the opposite end.

STEP 2

Rotate the paper 90-degrees to the left and valley-fold it in half away from you.

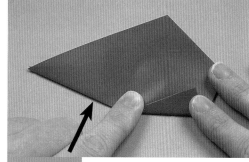

STEP 3

Fold a small flap over at the right-angled corner. Crease firmly and slowly, since the paper has several layers.

STEP 4

Unfold to the kite base and begin to form a rabbit's ear using the two halves of the central diamond creases that are nearest to you. The paper does not lie flat!

HELP!

Many of the steps are three-dimensional and must be folded off the table, so keep checking the next photo to see what you are aiming for.

RABBIT'S EAR FOLD REMINDER

Follow the simple folding instructions to Step 6, then rotate the point toward you and lift the paper, causing a verticle point to form. Flatten the point to one side.

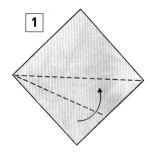

1

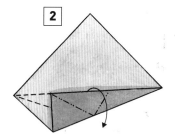

2

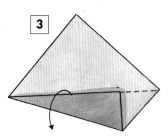

3

STEP 5

When the rabbit's ear is complete, start to bring its tip toward you.

STEP 6

Press in the center of the half diamond shape as you swing the sharp corner inward on the crease made in Step 1.

STEP 7

The paper will collapse naturally into this form. Blunt the tips of the outer corners by folding them in slightly...

STEP 8

...and the corners on the top.

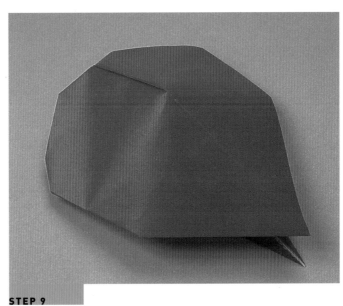

STEP 9

Turn the paper over to see the completed heart.

47

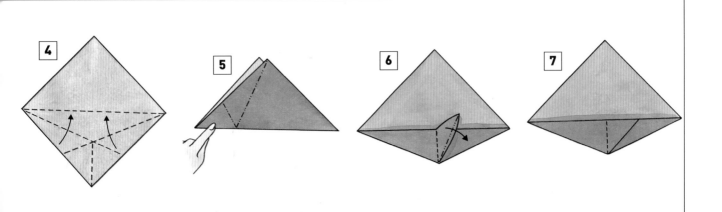

BOUTONNIERE

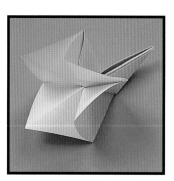

THIS TRADITIONAL DESIGN is a classic—simple, elegant, and beautiful. Many folders believe it is harder to capture a subject using simple lines than it is to create a more complex design with lots of detail. The boutonniere is an example of "climactic" folding, in which the final object is seen only at the last moment.

Try to find paper that is green on one side and a brighter color on the other. Spray adhesive is ideal for gluing two sheets together, but it must be used in a well-ventilated room.

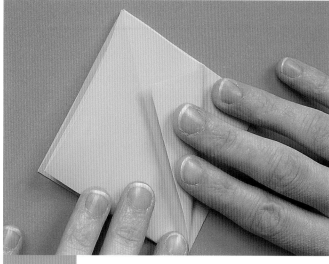

STEP 1

Start with a preliminary base, with the color of the petals inside. Turn the base so that the open ends are facing away from you. Fold one of the sides with folded edges to lie along the vertical center crease.

STEP 2

Repeat on the adjacent flap.

PRELIMINARY BASE REMINDER

Start with a waterbomb base and open it out. Put a finger underneath the paper and pop the folds up. Pinch the creases as they form a "+" shape and then flatten into two flaps.

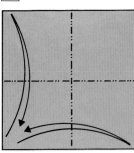

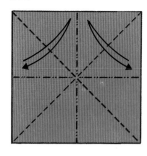

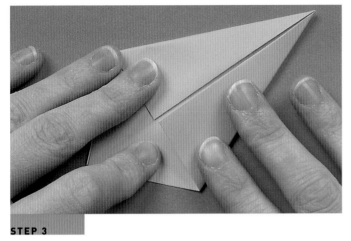

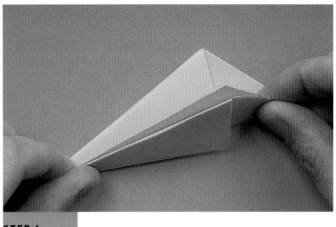

STEP 3

Then turn the paper over and fold both flaps to match.

STEP 4

Carefully fold the whole model in half along the center crease.

HELP!

When first making this design, you can add pre-creases for the reverse fold. Once you see what you are aiming for, try making it directly, as suggested (see Step 5).

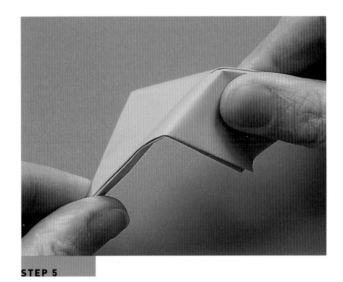

STEP 5

Turn the paper around so the longest edge is on top. Holding it in the air, pull the narrow point downward, adding an inside reverse fold directly into the paper. We don't pre-crease this fold because the paper is too thick. Use the next picture as a guide.

49

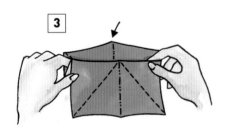

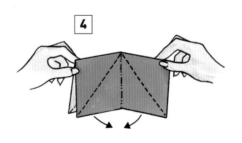

stage three **PROJECT**

STEP 6

When the reverse fold is in place, crease it firmly.

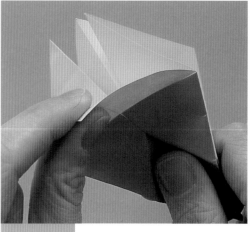

STEP 7

Hold the paper loosely, then start to peel back
the corner of the uppermost triangular flap.

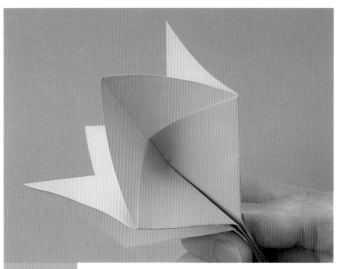

STEP 8

As you peel it back, the four petals suddenly spring out. Tighten
the reverse fold again.

INSIDE REVERSE FOLD REMINDER

**Just the last two steps
shown here. Ease the
paper gently back along
the fold lines to "reverse"
the fold.**

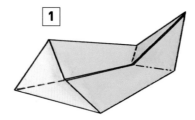

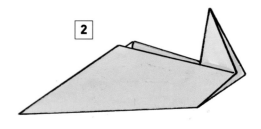

CARP

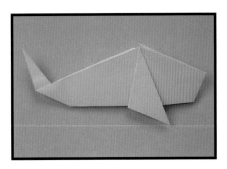

IN JAPAN, the carp symbolizes the will to succeed. On All Children's Day (May 5th), children make paper streamers from this basic design. This is one of the many simple models that can be made, not surprisingly, from a fish base! Some origami fish are highly detailed, but this one is a very basic but appealing design. The fold lines for this design have been provided on one of the practice sheets.

Using the carp as a starting point, can you create a fish of your own?

52

STEP 1

Start with a fish base. Lift the top flap and flatten the paper into a diamond.

STEP 2

Fold the diamond in half along the long center crease.

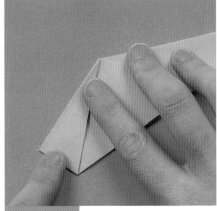

STEP 3

Take the right-hand point to the shallow point at the top. Crease firmly and unfold.

HELP!

If you make all pre-creases firmly, your reverse folds will be easier.

FISH BASE REMINDER

Start with an upside down kite base. Fold the sharp point to the opposite end, crease and turn over. Open the pockets and line up the center edges neatly.

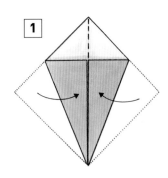

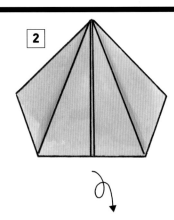

STEP 4

Then, make an inside reverse fold on that same crease.

STEP 5

There will now be two small triangular flaps. Fold each one to slightly past the verticle mark.

STEP 6

Fold the tip of the tail upward at a slight angle, crease and unfold.

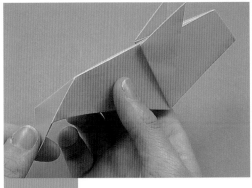

STEP 7

Form the tail using an inside reverse fold.

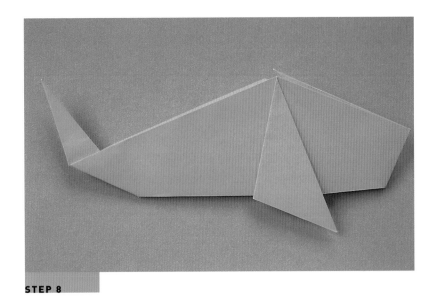

STEP 8

The completed carp.

53

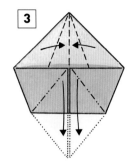

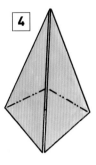

stage two **PRACTICE PIECE**

PAJARITA

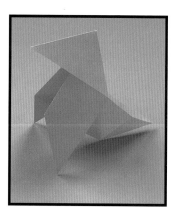

THE PAJARITA (Spanish for "little bird") has been an traditional symbol in Spain for many years. You can find it on airplanes, salt shakers, and even bars of chocolate! In origami, it is one of a long series of folds that uses the windmill base. The outside reverse fold that forms the head is also known as a "color-change," since it reveals the opposite side of the paper.

After you have completed the pajarita, unfold it and look carefully at the crease pattern. Try to work out how each crease is used in the final model. Analyzing crease patterns is a great help in creating new designs.

STEP 1
Start with a windmill base. Fold the top-left corner upward.

STEP 2
Mountain-fold the model in half, by folding the top-right corner behind to meet the bottom-left corner while pulling upward the top-left corner folded in Step 1.

STEP 3
This is the result.

WINDMILL BASE REMINDER

Start with a preliminary base opened out. Follow the simple folding steps until Step 5. Pull the triangular flaps until the paper flattens and forms a point on each side.

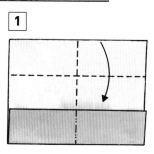

1

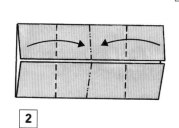

2

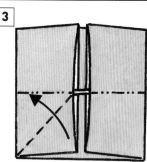

3

54

STEP 4

Begin to separate the layers at the top corner...

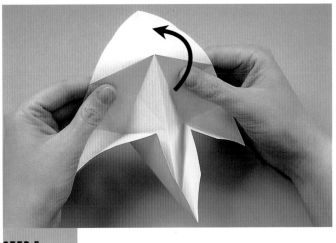

STEP 5

...then flip the corner inside out with an outside reverse fold.

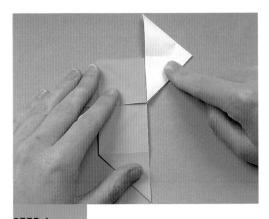

STEP 6

Flatten the head section, which will have a color change.

HELP!

Open the paper out as much as possible when forming the head—it will refold easily—if you have made the creases firmly (Step 5).

STEP 7

Separate the two front "wings" slightly to stand it up. The completed "pajarita."

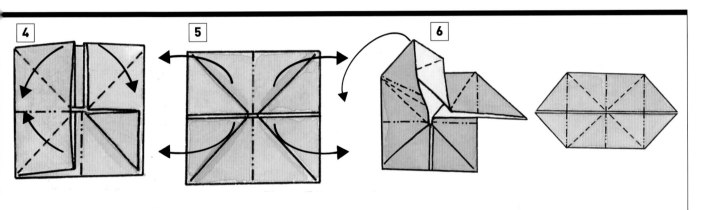

CUBE

THIS CLASSIC TOY has existed for many years and is well-known to schoolchildren as the "waterbomb" from which the base gets its name. However, it also forms an attractive fold for displaying on a mobile, particularly when it is folded from brightly colored paper.

HELP!

When tucking the flaps in to keep the model together, try to slip the paper neatly inside the pocket (Steps 6 and 7).

56

STEP 1

Start with a waterbomb base with the raw edges toward you. Fold a bottom corner to the top of the triangle.

STEP 2

Fold the top of the triangle to the bottom, making a location crease at the halfway point. Unfold this flap.

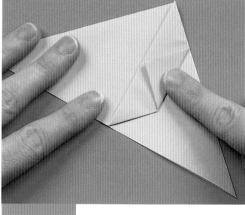

STEP 3

Fold the outside corner of the triangle to meet the location crease at the center of the paper. Repeat with the other corner on this side and the two corners underneath.

WATERBOMB BASE REMINDER

Fold paper in half horizontally, vertically, and diagonally. Holding the paper underneath, gently press it into a star shape. Then flatten into a triangle with two flaps.

1

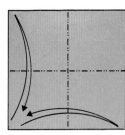

2

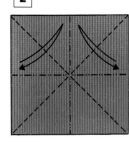

STEP 4

There are loose corners at the top of the model. Fold them down to the center to form a small triangle, twice on each side.

STEP 5

Fold the same triangle outward across the inside edge of the larger triangle, crease, and unfold.

STEP 6

Using the latest crease, begin to tuck the small triangle into the pocket of the larger triangle...

STEP 7

...like this. Repeat with the three other triangles.

57

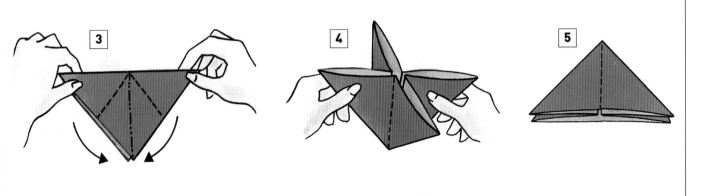

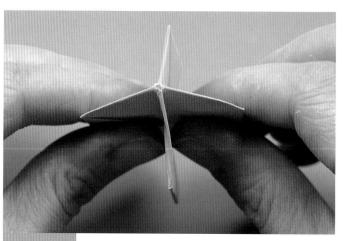

STEP 9

Spread the four flaps out to form a cross; then, holding two opposite flaps, blow into the small opening at the top of the model. As it inflates, use your fingers to help shape it into a rounded form.

STEP 8

Fold the nearest corner to the center, crease firmly and unfold. Repeat this action on the other corner.

58

STEP 10

Pinch the edges to make the form into a cube shape.

LOCATION CREASE REMINDER

Fold the paper in half vertically and unfold. Then fold the bottom to the top but only make a very small crease in the center.

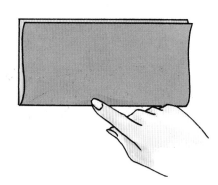

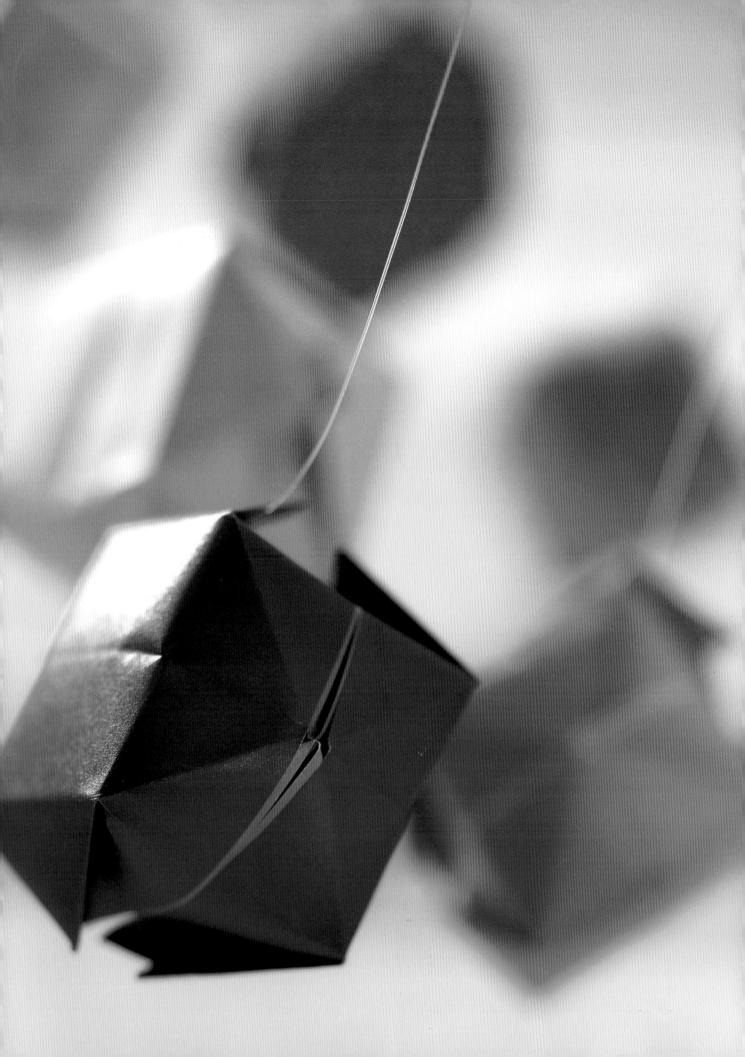

DISH

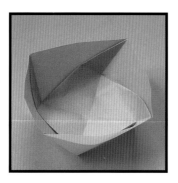

CREATED BY THE AUTHOR, this dish uses a simple locking technique to form the sides. The creases for this are done in advance, a technique known as "pre-creasing." You should make sure all pre-creasing is accurate. The fold lines for this design have been provided on one of the practice sheets.

Try to achieve smooth curves around the outside edges of the dish. By folding the mirror image of all the creases, you could create a dish that "twists" the other way.

STEP 3

Make a crease that joins the top right outside corner with the center of your practice paper.

STEP 1

Start with a square divided into sixteen smaller squares. Fold the nearest edge over to the center crease.

STEP 2

Fold the same edge over again, using the halfway crease. Then rotate the paper 180-degrees.

STEP 4

Unfold and fold the short raw edges on the right to meet the most recent crease made.

HELP!

If you struggle with the final lock, fold and unfold each corner in turn, so the paper knows where it is going.

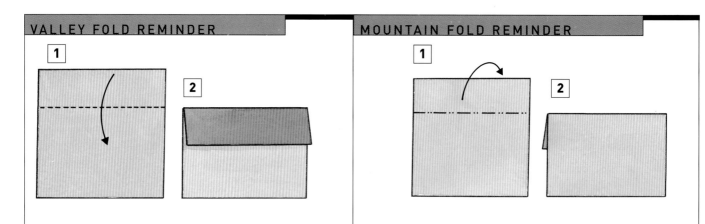

VALLEY FOLD REMINDER

1

2

MOUNTAIN FOLD REMINDER

1

2

STEP 5

Open the paper out and repeat Steps 1 through 4 on the three other edges. Unfold once more, turn the paper over and fold in using the valley crease indicated below the right-hand thumb.

STEP 6

Lock it into place by folding the small triangle behind.

STEP 7

Repeat the previous two steps on the other three corners. Take care with the final corner.

STEP 8

Turn the dish over and smooth all its creases to give it a slightly circular feel.

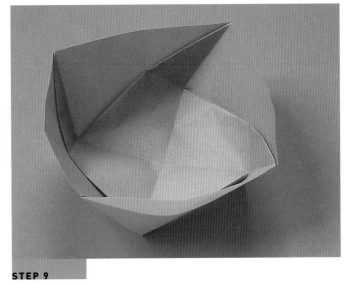

STEP 9

The completed dish.

LOCATION CREASE REMINDER

Fold the paper in half vertically and unfold. Then fold the bottom to the top but only make a very small crease at the fold mark at the center of the paper.

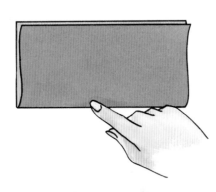

VALENTINE VASE

THIS DESIGN is by Pam Bisman from New Zealand. Note how the completed model holds itself together using the tension of the paper rather than complicated folding techniques. As with all origami, this design will look best if you fold neatly and accurately. It is interesting to see how the straight line creases can produce a model which appears to have curves.

Since the model incorporates a heart motif, you may want to use red or pink paper.

HELP!

Opening the layers is easiest if you do it in the air (Step 5).

STEP 1

Start with a windmill base, unfolded back to the original square. Alternatively, fold all quarter creases, then take each corner to the center and unfold. Fold a corner in to the first intersection of creases.

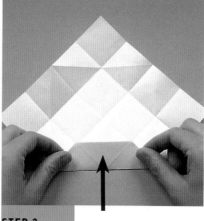

STEP 2

Fold over again on an existing crease. Repeat with the other three corners.

STEP 3

Take a corner to the opposite corner of the smaller internal square, but only crease the thinner central section.

WINDMILL BASE REMINDER

Start with a preliminary base opened back to the square. Follow the simple folding steps until Step 5. Then pull the triangular flaps at one end until the paper flattens and forms a point. Repeat steps on the other end.

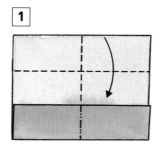

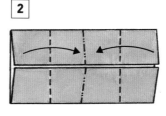

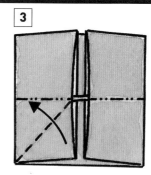

62

STEP 4

Repeat on the other three sides, then turn the paper over and fold all four corners to the center.

STEP 5

Turn over once more, then open out one of the pockets with your finger, gently pressing the sides together.

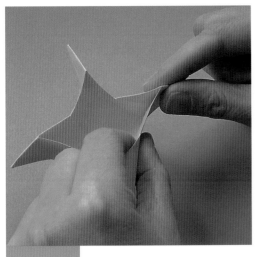

STEP 6

Repeat with the other three corners. The creases made in Steps 3 and 4 form the base of the vase.

STEP 7

The completed vase.

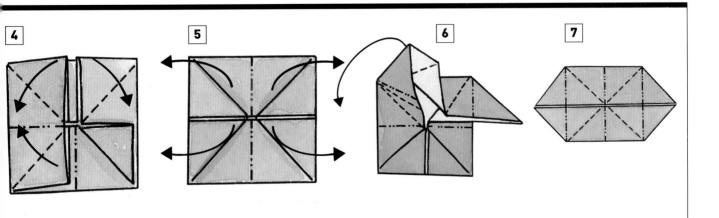

BOOKMARK

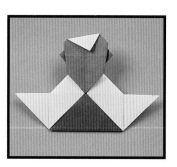

SINCE A BOOKMARK is such a simple concept (basically just a triangular pocket), it is a great subject to use when creating your first original models. Many will be purely functional, but this design adds a head and arms to make the bookmark more fun.

The folds that shape the hair and ears can be varied to suit your own taste.

64

STEP 1

Start with a preliminary base, opened out to a square. The "head" color should be toward you. Fold each corner to the center, crease firmly, then unfold.

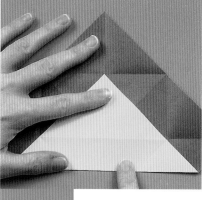

STEP 2

Fold each corner to the opposite quarter crease, crease firmly, then unfold. Leave the final crease in place.

HELP!

This design is quite challenging, so study the instructions and photographs carefully to fully understand each step. Be sure to tuck in the final flap carefully, or the paper may crumple (Step 15).

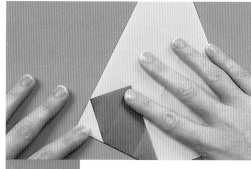

STEP 3

Turn the paper over and fold the left-hand corner to the center of the paper (where the creases meet).

PRELIMINARY BASE REMINDER

Start with a waterbomb base and open it out. Put a finger underneath and pop the folds up. Pinch the creases as they form a "+" shape and then flatten into two flaps.

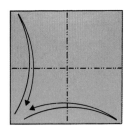

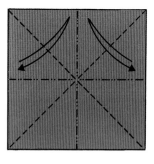

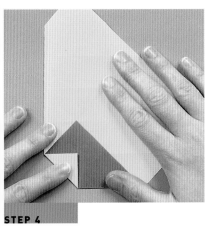

STEP 4

Fold the small triangle inward, crease firmly and unfold.

STEP 5

Make a valley fold using the crease at the center of the triangle, carefully squash-folding the corner. Repeat Steps 3 to 5 on the right-hand side.

STEP 6

Turn the paper over and inside reverse fold the right-hand outer section. The "arm" pops out during this step. Check the next photo as a guide. Repeat on the left-hand side.

STEP 7

Precrease and form a waterbomb base (see reminder below) in the top square section.

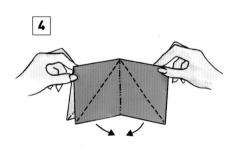

STEP 8

Turn the paper over and fold the two corners behind the head in toward the original center of the square.

STEP 9

Make two small pleats to form the ears—try to make them the same.

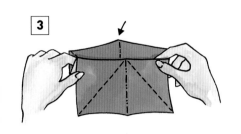

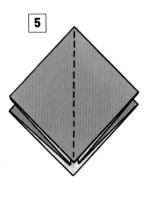

stage three PROJECT

STEP 10

Turn the paper over and put your fingers inside the flaps of the body (as shown in inset), then open them fully out and squash-fold away from you. Fold the original corner to the first intersection of creases...

STEP 11

...then fold the flap over again on an existing crease (see inset). Pull down the top flap of the boat-shaped section, flattening the paper toward you. The result is shown in the main photo.

66

STEP 12

Fold a small corner down to form the hair and flatten all the creases. Your bookmark is complete!

SQUASH FOLD BASE REMINDER

Start with a square that has been folded in half. After folding to the center, separate the two layers and "squash" the fold. Be sure to line up the squashed fold with the center crease.

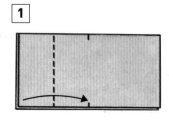

1

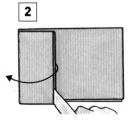

2

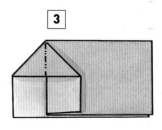

3

CHRISTMAS TREE

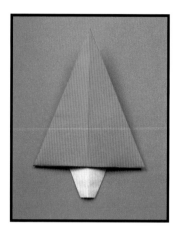

ONE OF THE SIMPLEST DESIGNS in this book, this charming tree is perfect for Christmas cards. If you make many trees, of varying sizes, they can be made into a realistic woodland montage. Altering the creases and rounding off the sharp points allows you to create several other types of tree. The fold lines for this design have been provided on one of the practice sheets.

HELP!

Because this design is so simple, you should concentrate on creating a perfect example every time!

STEP 1

Start with an upside-down kite base. Fold a small tip of the original corner inward.

STEP 2

Fold a short raw edge to the center crease. Repeat on the other side.

KITE BASE REMINDER

Start with a diagonal crease and fold one side in to line up with the center crease. Repeat on the other side.

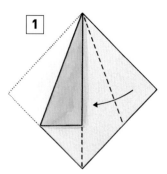

1

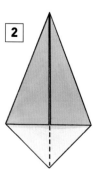

2

68

STEP 3

Fold in half between the widest corners, creasing firmly.

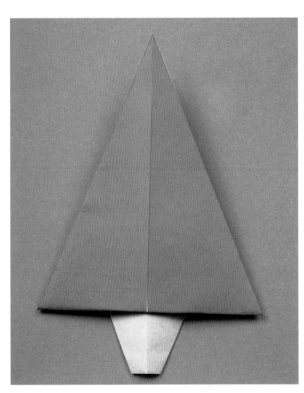

STEP 4

Valley-fold the blunt end back down so that half of it lies past the folded edge.

STEP 5

Turn the piece over to see the completed Christmas tree.

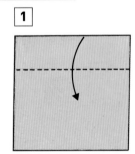

VALLEY FOLD REMINDER

To make a valley fold, simply fold the paper toward you and make a firm crease.

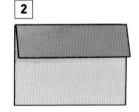

ENVELOPE

ENVELOPES HAVE BEEN USED for hundreds of years and much research has been carried out to study their history and use. There is even a group called ELFA (Envelope and Letter Folding Association) which publishes collections of envelope designs. The aim is always to create a practical design that keeps its contents secure. The fold lines for this design have been provided on one of the practice sheets.

Almost all the creases in this design can be altered to some extent. Try as many variations as you can think of.

STEP 1
Start with a square with both diagonals creased. Valley-fold a corner to the center, crease and unfold.

70

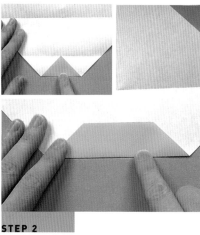

STEP 2
Make a similar fold placing the corner at the last crease made (as shown in inset). Fold this flap over on the existing crease.

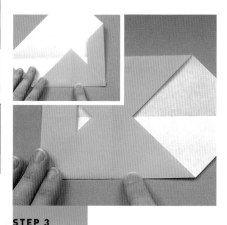

STEP 3
Rotate the paper to the position shown (see inset), then fold the corner inward to a point just past the center point. Turn the paper around and repeat on the opposite side. The two raw edges meet over the center crease.

HELP!

Start with a larger square if you plan to mail your envelope!

VALLEY FOLD REMINDER

To make a valley fold, simply fold the paper toward you and make a firm crease.

1

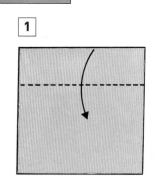

2

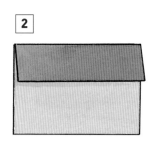

STEP 4
Fold the remaining corner to lie along the raw edges.

STEP 5
Rotate the paper 180-degrees and fold the same corner back out to the center of the top edge.

STEP 6
Then mountain-fold the whole of the loose flap behind on the crease made in Step 4.

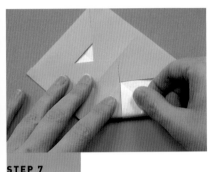

STEP 7
Fold a corner of the same edge to where the raw edges meet. Repeat with the other corner.

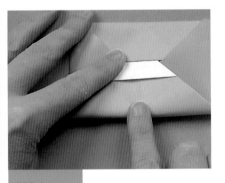

STEP 8
Carefully fold the pointed flap inside the small pocket.

STEP 9
Finally, press the fold flat and turn it around to see the completed envelope.

MOUNTAIN FOLD REMINDER

To make a mountain fold, simply fold the paper away from you and make a firm crease.

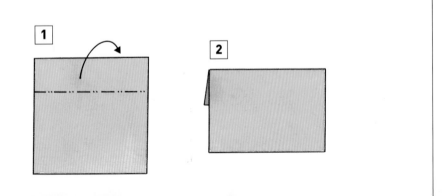

stage three PROJECT

SANTA

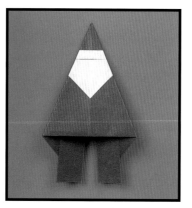

THIS DESIGN WAS CREATED by Minako Ishibashi from Japan. It is a fine example of how you can use origami to suggest a subject rather than to make a perfect copy of it; this Santa is clearly recognizable even with a minimum of features.

HELP!

Take care when narrowing the body at the final stages —the thicker layers of paper will crumple if you are not careful.

STEP 1

Start with a square that has a diagonal crease. Fold one end of the diagonal to the other and make a small location crease in the center and unfold (see inset). Then, fold a corner to the center (main picture).

STEP 2

Turn the paper over and fold half of the short edge to the center crease.

STEP 3

Repeat the same fold on the other side of the short edge.

VALLEY FOLD REMINDER

To make a valley fold, simply fold the paper toward you and make a firm crease.

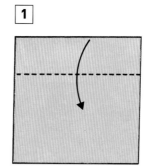

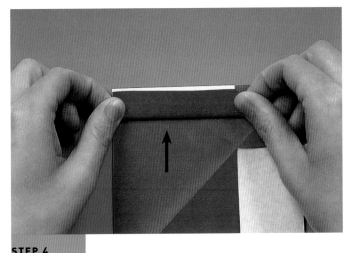

STEP 4

Fold the short edge in half back toward the outer edge so that only one color is visible.

STEP 5

Repeat the previous step on the opposite side.

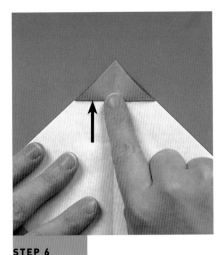

STEP 6

Turn the paper over and fold the inside corner of the small square to the outside corner. Crease firmly and unfold again.

STEP 7

Fold the same corner to the center of the square (see new foldmark).

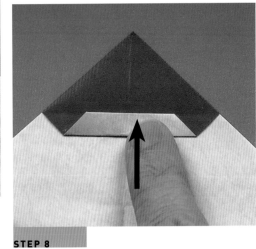

STEP 8

Fold the small triangle in half...

73

MOUNTAIN FOLD REMINDER

To make a mountain fold, simply fold the paper away from you and make a firm crease.

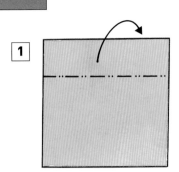

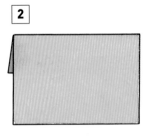

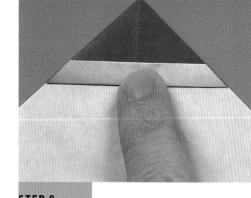

STEP 9

...then fold over again on the crease made in Step 5.

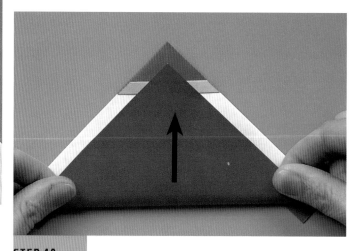

STEP 10

Fold the original corner to meet the opposite corner.

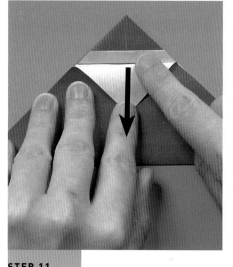

STEP 11

Fold the beard down just below the lining of the hat.

STEP 12

Turn over and fold a long edge to meet the center crease.

STEP 13

Repeat on the other side, pressing the model flat. The completed Santa!

LOCATION CREASE REMINDER

Fold the paper in half vertically and unfold. Then fold the bottom to the top but only make a very small crease in the center.

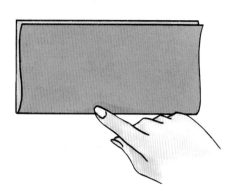

74

WOODPECKER

ORIGAMI MODELS that have some kind of movement or action have always been popular with both adults and children. This design uses a familiar technique for creating movement. The position and angle of the beak can be varied to taste. If you fold from crisp paper, quite a loud peck can be heard. The fold lines for this design have been provided on one of the practice sheets.

With just a few changes you can create a snapping beak instead. Try to come up with your own designs.

STEP 1

Start with an upside-down diamond base. Starting at the left-hand corner, fold the right-hand edge back along itself, but only crease as far as the center. Repeat on the left-hand side.

STEP 2

Turn the paper all the way around, then make the same folds at the other end. This will form a diamond-shaped crease pattern at the center.

HELP!

It is important to make all the creases sharp and neat for the best "pecking" action. Try to use crisp paper.

STEP 3

Turn the paper over and unfold two flaps at one end of the diamond base. Either end is fine. Fold both outside corners in to meet the two inner corners and crease firmly.

INSIDE REVERSE FOLD REMINDER

Start with a kite base. All the necessary folds are present by Step 5, but they must change direction. Ease the paper gently back along the fold lines to "reverse" the fold.

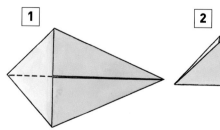

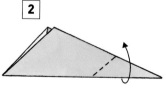

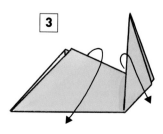

STEP 4

Pick the paper up and reinforce the diamond-shaped creases made in Steps 1 and 2 so that they pass through the extra layers.

STEP 5

Make an inside reverse fold to form a beak.

STEP 6

Fold either side of the beak downward, creasing firmly.

STEP 7

Hold the model by both sides (see inset) and gently press together to make the completed woodpecker peck!

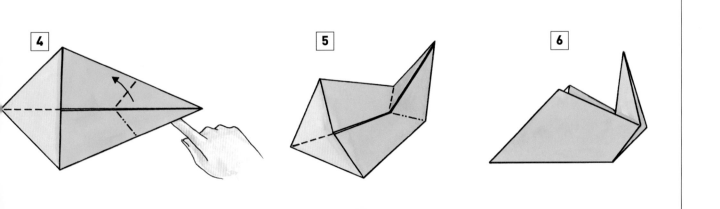

stage two PRACTICE PIECE

FLAPPING BIRD

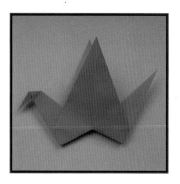

PERHAPS THE BEST known origami model after the paper airplane, this classic fold has been known for at least 150 years, possibly longer. The flapping action is guaranteed to enchant both children and adults whenever they see it. It can be folded quite rapidly with practice; the author made over 1,000 in a single day while raising money for charity! The fold lines for this design have been provided on one of the practice sheets.

78

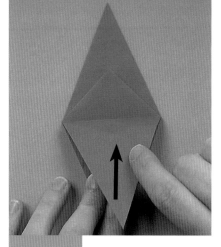

STEP 1
Start with a bird base. Fold the rear and front flaps upward.

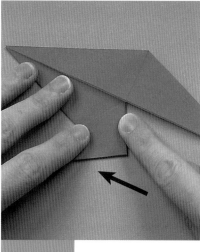

STEP 2
There are two thin flaps; fold one upward at an angle, starting from the center of the paper. Use later pictures as guides. Crease firmly!

HELP!

The tricky part is teaching the bird to flap. Try to curl the wings to encourage them to move and never pull too hard or too quickly.

STEP 3
Make an inside reverse fold using the crease you have just made. Repeat with the other thin flap.

BIRD BASE REMINDER

Start with a preliminary base. After Step 2, turn over and repeat. Unfold two flaps and lift the top flap to complete Steps 5 and 6. Turn over and repeat last two steps.

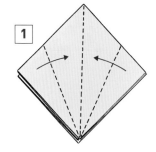

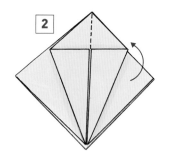

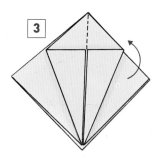

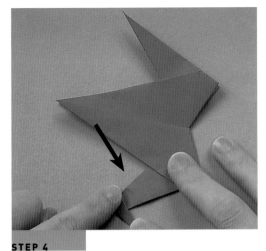

STEP 4

Fold a small section of one point over to form a beak. Crease firmly and unfold.

STEP 5

Make an inside reverse fold on that crease.

STEP 6

The completed flapping bird is ready for flight!

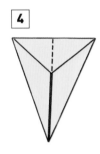

4

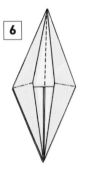

5

6

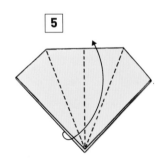

7

ACROBAT

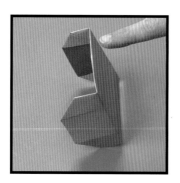

THIS DELIGHTFUL TOY was created by the late Seiro Takekawa, a Japanese folder who specialized in simple folds for children. The tumbling action seems simple also, but if you don't know the trick you won't be able to make it work every time!

The narrowing of the edges in Steps 4 and 5 needs to be quite precise for the fold to perform effectively.

HELP!

It doesn't matter if the edges overlap slightly in Step 7. The edges should be exactly at right angles for the fold to perform effectively (Step 8).

STEP 1

Start with a square, colored side up. Fold the square in half, then open out.

STEP 2

Fold both edges in to the center crease, opening one out again.

80

VALLEY FOLD REMINDER

To make a valley fold, simply fold the paper toward you and crease firmly.

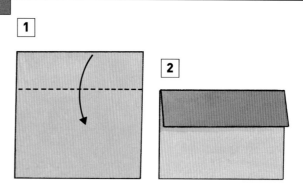

1

2

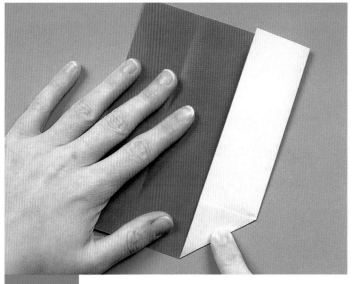

STEP 3

Fold both corners of the white section in to meet the inside edge.
Repeat with the opposite side, folding the corners to meet the
quarter crease.

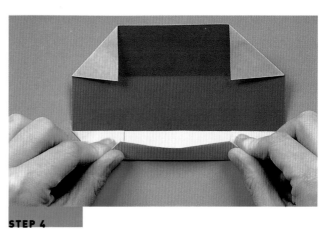

STEP 4

Lift the outside folded edge in to meet the inside raw edge.
Hold the corners in place as you flatten the crease.

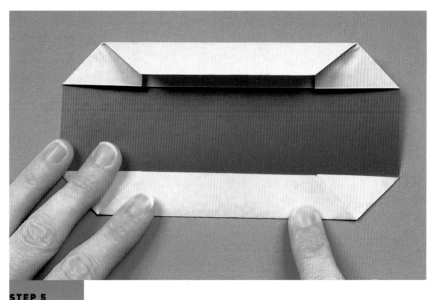

STEP 5

Turn the paper around and make a similar fold on the other edge.

To make a mountain
fold, simply fold the
paper away from you
and crease firmly.

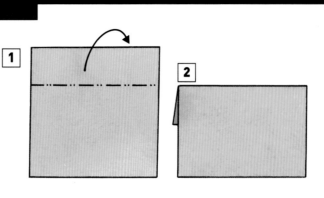

STEP 7

Rotate the paper again and repeat the fold with the other short edge.

STEP 6

Turn the paper sideways and fold the short edge in to the center. The crease lies along hidden edges of paper and so is easy to locate.

STEP 8

Open the short edges to halfway and stand the paper on its side, with the thicker side (it has double the layers) on top. Gently tip the paper over with your fingertip and it will perform a somersault. The trick is to then pick it up with the thinner side on top and invite your friend to try the same thing.

DIAMOND BASE REMINDER

Start with a kite base and fold both of the shorter edges to the center.

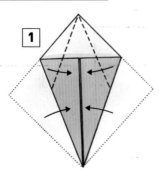

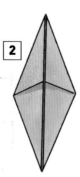

LIVELY CREATURES

THE WORLD OF NATURE has always been a rich source of inspiration for artists, and paper folders are no exception. Certain creatures, such as penguins, elephants, and dogs, are very popular, whereas others, such as slugs, hamsters, and cows, are very uncommon. Over the past few years there has been a growing interest in origami dinosaurs, including a number of skeletons! When creating your own designs, try to explore subjects that are not as common. That way, you are more likely to arrive at an original concept.

CHICK
A classic design by Kunihiko Kasahara.

DRAGON
This mythical dragon by Robert Neale is created from the humble bird base.

GOLDFISH
One of the few designs that is inflated into shape by blowing inside it!

THURBER DOG
Created by Robert Neale
in the early 1960s.

BABY BIRD
An original design by
the author showing
a baby bird in a nest.

SATSUMA'S DOG
A charming design by
Fred Satsuma created
in the 1990s.

SNAIL
This crawling snail is a
traditional variation of
the bird base.

DISHES & BOXES

DISHES AND BOXES are the perfect challenge for origami folders—their methods are usually quite straightforward, and you can tell immediately whether you have been successful. Some containers are more decorative, with gentle curves and a pleasing elegance of shape, while others are purely practical. There are probably more origami designs in these subject areas than any others.

STUDIO 2
Inspired by the elegant lines of 1950s Hornsea Pottery.

LOUIS'S BOX
This box has a more complex design that "weaves" the sides together.

DECORATIVE DISH
A practical dish with decorative edges.

CLASSIC DISH
A classic design by
Philip Shen.

MINIMAL DISH
Here we see how minimal
folding can produce
beautiful lines.

DRINKING CUP
A sturdy and practical cup
by Paulo Mulatinho.

FACES & GEOMETRIC SHAPES

ORIGAMI FACES CAN BE simple or complex, but you should concentrate on the main features of the eyes, nose, and mouth for the best effects. Alongside the faces are some classic geometric shapes created by origami masters.

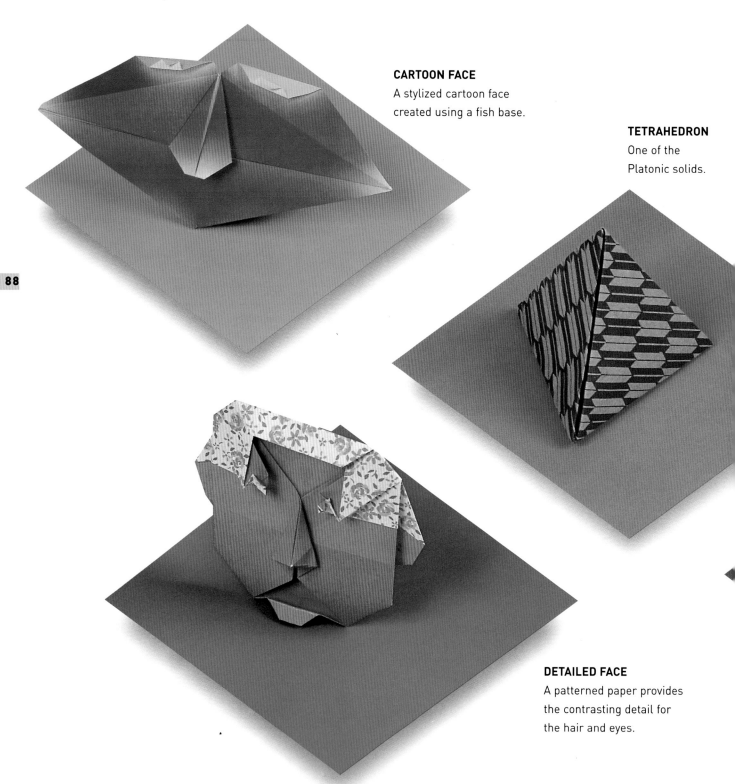

CARTOON FACE
A stylized cartoon face created using a fish base.

TETRAHEDRON
One of the Platonic solids.

DETAILED FACE
A patterned paper provides the contrasting detail for the hair and eyes.

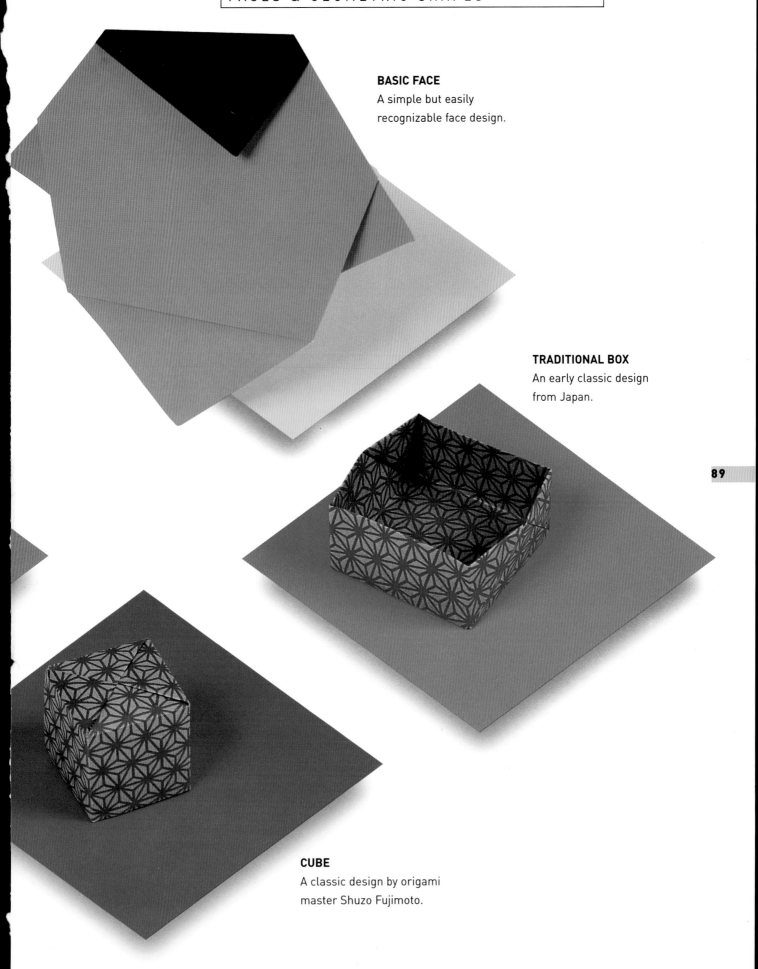

BASIC FACE
A simple but easily
recognizable face design.

TRADITIONAL BOX
An early classic design
from Japan.

CUBE
A classic design by origami
master Shuzo Fujimoto.

UNIQUE & FUN SHAPES

THIS COLLECTION OF ORIGAMI designs reflects the varied nature of paperfolding. No subject is beyond the reach of a talented folder, and it is common for a shape to have some kind of personal connection to its designer. Think about your own personal interests and see if you are inspired to create a new design!

BOOK
This little book by Martin Wall is a variation of a simple box.

TRADITIONAL CHURCH
A simple design from a waterbomb base.

SAMURI HELMET
Another traditional design from Japan.

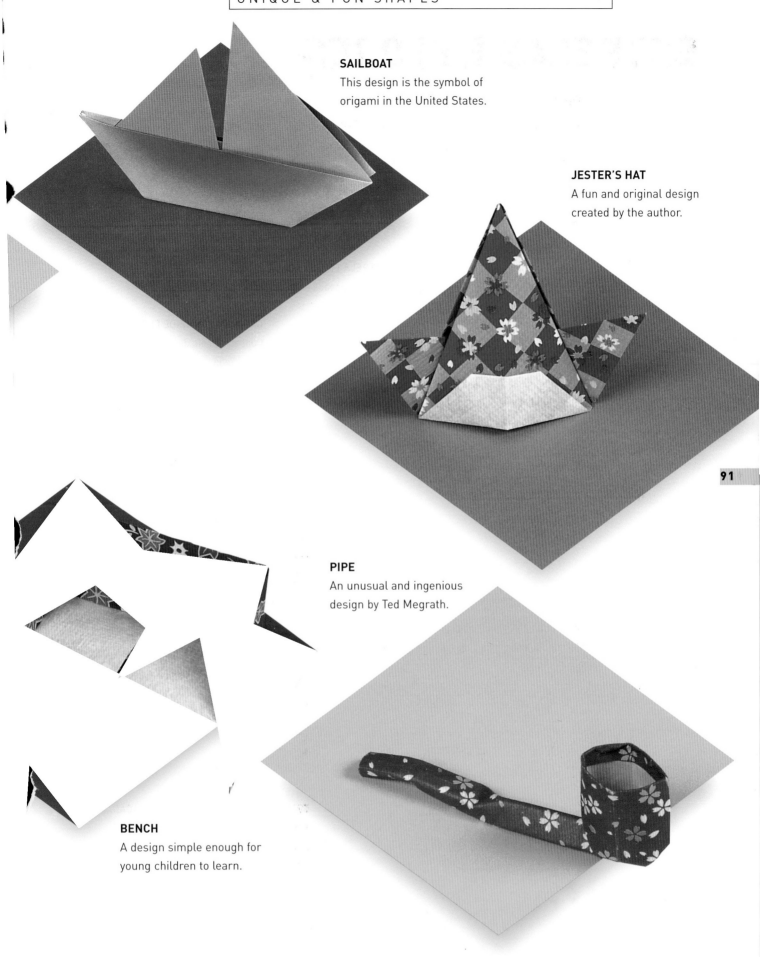

SAILBOAT
This design is the symbol of origami in the United States.

JESTER'S HAT
A fun and original design created by the author.

PIPE
An unusual and ingenious design by Ted Megrath.

BENCH
A design simple enough for young children to learn.

91

STARS & FLOWERS

IF YOU USE THE same technique on each corner of a square, you are likely to arrive at a regular shape, such as a star or flower. These designs lend themselves to many variations in shape and color pattern, producing designs that are usually very eye-catching.

TWISTED STAR
Based on a division of the paper into thirds.

BOX PETAL FLOWER
Created by the Danish master Thoki Yenn.

TWISTED SQUARE STAR
This example uses "duo" toned paper to create an interesting pattern.

SIMPLE FLOWER
A flower design also known
as the Fortune Teller.

OPEN BLOSSOM FLOWER
One of Philip Shen's
masterpieces.

TWISTED STAR
This design utilizes both
sides of the paper to create
contrast.

INDEX

CREDITS

The following origami designs were created by these artists:

Star ring by Robert Neale, page 30; dish by Nick Robinson, page 60; Valentine vase by Pam Bisman, page 62; bookmark by Nick Robinson, page 64, Santa by Minako Ishibashi, page 72; acrobat by Seiro Takeawa, page 80; chick by Kunihiko Kasahara, page 84; dragon by Robert Neale, page 84; baby bird by Nick Robinson, page 85; Thurber Dog by Robert Neale, page 85; Satsuma's dog by Fred Satsuma, page 85; classic dish by Philip Shen, page 87; drinking cup by Paulo Mulatinho, page 87; cube by Shuzo Fujimoto, page 89; book by Martin Wall, page 90; jester's hat by Nick Robinson, page 91; pipe by Ted Megrath, page 90; box petal flower by Thoki Yenn, page 92; open blossom flower by Philip Shen, page 93.

INTERNATIONAL ORIGAMI ASSOCIATIONS

Origami is an art you can study on your own, but it's also a lot of fun to fold as part of a group! Here are two major origami organizations:

Origami USA (OUSA)
15 West 77th Street
New York, NY 10024-5192
USA
email: www.origami-usa.org

David Brill
British Origami Society
35 Corfe Crescent Hazel Grove
Stockport
Cheshire SK7 5PR
Tel: 0161 456 9975
email: www.rpmrecords.co.uk/bos